TUMULT AND ORDER

Malcontenta 1924–1939

ANTONIO FOSCARI

TUMULT
AND ORDER

MALCONTENTA 1924–1939

Translated by Lucinda Byatt

LARS MÜLLER PUBLISHERS

To Ferigo and Giulia

Cover image:
Baroness Catherine d'Erlanger and Oliver Messel, Villa Foscari (photo: Cecil Beaton)
Cover colors: Le Corbusier no. 32081 (cover); no. 32033 (inside of cover)

Introduction

Bertie Landsberg regarded me as a descendant of one of the two Foscari brothers for whom Andrea Palladio built a villa at Malcontenta in the mid-16th century. Their names are carved on the frieze below the pediment of its porticoed façade. For my part, I was so absorbed in my life as an architecture student that I listened with extreme interest to everything that this kind gentleman told me about this superb building. What was more, he gave me an insight into a unique manner of preserving a historic monument that he had developed over the many years he had lived there and through his countless conversations with the stream of visitors to the villa.

In short, I knew little about Bertie as an individual. My impression of him was that he usually wore a rather tattered white linen suit and he never missed an opportunity to welcome visitors, even if it required laboriously climbing the narrow stairs to the main door. For the rest, his cosmopolitanism, his natural elegance, and his humor all created an aura, but to me his character remained largely an enigma. After Bertie's death, Claud Phillimore never spoke to me about him, except in a few brief remarks that failed to whet my curiosity. To Claud my lack of interest may have seemed inexplicable when, at the end of an extraordinary series of events for which Claud was responsible, Barbara and I had the good fortune and responsibility of living in this house.

At least, I imagine this is what Claud thought when, one rainy day, he rang the doorbell of our home and handed me a parcel, wrapped in thick yellow paper and containing a book. "A present?" I asked, slightly surprised. "More than that," he replied, giving me one of his characteristic smiles. Inside the package was the visitors' book that Bertie had kept throughout the years he lived at La Malcontenta. For a few minutes Claud stood watching me as I turned the pages of what to me was then just a mysterious collection of signatures. He nodded when I noted how the handwriting changed after the War: before it the signatures were peremptory, afterwards they were minute, almost timid. Then Claud left as discreetly as he had arrived.

Only over the following years did I understand that the book was more than a gift, as he had said. It was like a sort of puzzle that, if I had the patience to complete it, would allow me to reconstruct Bertie's life and discover more of his personality through the people who had visited him. That Serge Diaghilev and Cole Porter should be among the first to visit Bertie at his house offers a glimpse of the cultural climate in which he embarked on his Palladian adventure. Diaghilev did not hesitate to install powerful floodlights illuminating the waters of the Grand Canal in front of Palazzo Papadopoli, while Cole Porter arranged for an all-black troupe to dance to the syncopated beat of the Charleston on a barge moored in front of Palazzo Rezzonico. The intensity of these lights and sounds eradicated any possible residue of the decadent romantic culture that still lingered after a century of unrivaled dominance over Venice and its lagoon. In these early years after the First World War, Venice was entering modernity with its port infrastructures, its new industries, its grand hotels, and the Art Biennale. Le Corbusier, who was in Venice for an international congress and to visit La Malcontenta, rightly said that it was the transfer of industrial activities to Marghera that assured the survival of the historic city. This focus on conservation was itself an aspect of modernity. In this sense the rigorous preservation of Palladio's architectural master-piece on the banks of the Brenta was also a conscious act of modernity. One could go even further to state that the villa acted as an alternative to the attractions of the Lido. Venice was a magnet for those artistic avant-gardes and intellectual elites who, mingling with the remnants of European aristocracy and a few highly eccentric members of the bour-geoisie, created the fertile social milieu from which modern art emerged. That Bertie had his portrait drawn by Pablo Picasso, while his sister was painted by Henri Matisse, should thus not come as a surprise.

It was not only the supreme quality of the Palladian architecture and the hospitality of the villa's owner that attracted these visitors, but also the singular *ménage à trois* who lived there. Bertie's very existence was indissolubly linked with those of both a French noblewoman of exceptional vitality, and a refined man of culture who was a uniquely talented interior designer. In all, life on the banks of the Brenta Riviera was such that, for a while, it was possible to overlook the worrying signs of the political crisis gathering in the heart of Europe.

Bertie Landsberg

Paul Rodocanachi

Yvonne Landsberg

Pablo Picasso   Jean Cocteau

Claud Phillimore

Coco Chanel (with Cecil Beaton)

Arturo-José
Lopez-Willshaw

Catherine d'Erlanger

Oliver Messel
(with Catherine
d'Erlanger)

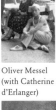

Misia Sert (with
Coco Chanel)

Boris Kochno

Serge Lifar,
Lydia Sokolova

Serge Diaghilev   Serge Lifar   Norah Lindsay

Alberto Giacometti, Jean-Michel Frank,
Emilio Terry, Paul Rodocanachi,
Christian Bérard, Adolphe Chanaux,
and Diego Giacometti

Roger Quilter

Igor Stravinsky (with Vera)

Lord Snowc

Paul Morand

Henri Matisse   Christian Bérard   Le Corbusier and
Antonio Foscari

10

Characters

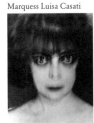
Marquess Luisa Casati

Cecil Beaton

Cole Porter

Linda Lee Thomas

Diana Cooper

Princess "Baba"
of Faucigny-Lucinge

Prince Jean-Louis
of Faucigny-Lucinge

Giuseppe Volpi

Anina Morosini

Marina Volpi

...axwell

Gerald Murphy, Jinny Carpenter,
Cole Porter and Sara Murphy

Jane Campbell,
Princess of
San Faustino

...Byron

Bruce Chatwin

Leo Castelli and Cy Twombly

Peggy Guggenheim

Andy Warhol

...Stark

Jannis Kounellis

Jean Tinguely (with Antonio Foscari)

Robert Rauschenberg

11

TUMULT AND ORDER

"I stood with Diana on the lawn below the portico, as the glow before dusk defined for one moment more clearly every stage of the design. Europe could have bid me no fonder farewell than this triumphant affirmation of the European intellect. [...] Inside, the candles were lit and Lifar danced."
Robert Byron, *The Road to Oxiana*

A Fall in the Park

Albert Clinton Landsberg fell off his horse while riding in the Bois de Boulogne in Paris—recounted Claud Phillimore in a light-hearted tone, punctuated by brief pauses.

The uncommonly handsome young man, unconscious, was carried by a gentleman who'd also been riding into a nearby house at Neuilly-sur-Seine (to be precise, Number 14 Rue du Centre). There, lying on a bed, he recovered sufficiently to state his name and nationality before losing consciousness again.

The man's face lit up in a smile as he leaned over the gentleman from an armchair drawn close to the bed. The surname Landsberg (which derived from a small German town), coupled with Brazilian nationality and a perfect English accent triggered—or more accurately illuminated—his imagination. All three were clues to the handsome young man's immediate past: clearly he had come to Paris from England.

The man in the armchair was **Paul Rodocanachi**. He was about forty years old at the time, and he carried himself with consummate elegance. His face was framed by hair that already revealed a hint of gray, while his penetrating gaze had an indefinable air of melancholy.

Paul was a descendant of a Jewish family from Chios, which had emigrated to Europe in 1821, fleeing from the harsh repression with which the Ottoman Empire planned to crush the nationalist spirit of the Greeks who had inhabited the island for centuries. (According to Claud, a member of the Rodocanachi family had commissioned Delacroix's huge painting, *The Massacre of Chios*, in 1824, re-evoking that dramatic event.)[1]

Paul was born in London in 1871. He had been brought up, along with his three sisters, in an enterprising and affluent milieu by their energetic mother. His cultured and refined manner, and the social relations that he maintained throughout his life, testified to the excellent education he had received at one of the top boarding schools.

From an early age he showed a particular inclination towards art, and to forms of enjoyment that he soon realized were frowned upon by the social and ethical rules of Victorian society. These constraints would have been even more stringently imposed had he remained in a family whose sole ambition was to see him join the banking business started a few years earlier by his father and his cousin Michael.

Paul Rodocanachi and the Agelasto relatives
Paul Rodocanachi, 1930s

Façade of the house in Rue du Centre, Paris, 1928 (drawing: Paul Rodocanachi)
Hôtel Rodocanachi, La cour d'honneur, August 1926
Bottom: Hôtel Rodocanachi, Rue du Centre, postcards, 1909 and 1915

The House in Rue du Centre

After mulling over the decision for some time, Paul finally
made up his mind to leave London following his father's death
at the end of 1899. Having inherited a considerable fortune,
he decided to move to Paris to be at the heart of the radical
and exciting intellectual fervor and the renewal of social
customs, which, at the turn of the century, sparked off a process of cultural change that affected the entire Western world.
His decision was certainly not opposed by his mother,
who had been born in Marseilles and was also keen to return
to France.

Once settled in Paris (at Number 81, Avenue Victor Hugo),
Paul dedicated himself to the study of architecture. Soon
he became so proficient in the use of his instruments, and so
precise in his drawing techniques (even when drafting by
hand), and he had acquired such control over proportion,
that many believed he had been trained by an excellent master.[2]

That Paul had no intention of obtaining a qualification
at the end of his studies—a step that would have enabled him
to work professionally—is not surprising. Nothing could have
been less akin to his approach to life than being paid for work
that he regarded as a vocation, or accepting some sort of
hierarchical relationship (as professional relations often are)
which might cramp his style.

In order not to go against that elitist attitude which
governed every step of his life, he decided to remain an amateur,
although he was well aware that this approach depended
largely on existential rather than cultural options. Indeed,
he could not accept that a profession might reduce or in some
way hinder the "gentleman's" way of life, which he had adopted
as an ideal social status. In short, he wanted to become
the heir to those French aristocrats who, in previous centuries,
had described themselves as *dilettanti* (using that useful
expression which Sebastiano Serlio had introduced to the
court of François I in the mid-sixteenth century).

——

It was in this spirit that, in September 1903, aged just over
thirty, he acquired half a hectare of land in Neuilly-sur-Seine,
on the corner of Rue du Centre and Rue de Longchamp,
in order to build himself a house, and so confirm his choice
of Paris as the epicenter of his life.[3]

Educating the Pupil

Within a month after signing, and aided by a professional architect to expedite the necessary bureaucracy, Paul presented the plans for a *hôtel avec dépendances* (private house with outbuildings), to stand between the two streets.[4]

The house, therefore, is not far from the Bois de Boulogne. As Claud told us, "It looks like a Louis XV *maison de plaisance* (house of leisure), with a Louis XVI extension, and it is a perfect blend of design and proportion." The upper floor, which was used for entertaining, is divided into two areas by a central gallery: one facing north to the Rue du Centre, and the other south, overlooking a vast garden that slopes gently northwards.[5]

Nothing about the house was banal. Each room was carefully proportioned, creating an atmosphere of elegance that was, in some respects, mysterious.

Paul's expertise as a designer was by no means limited to the field of architecture: indeed, it also encompassed the "decorative arts," a sphere in which he excelled. He designed every one of the objects and decorative features that made up the "intimate landscape" which **Albert Clinton Landsberg**, who was known as Bertie by his friends, discovered when he regained consciousness.

With that special tact that was always Claud's distinguishing trait, whenever he referred to this long-ago event, he liked to make out that Bertie's convalescence following his fall lasted a very long time. Indeed, Bertie—having discovered a man whose cultured background and learning was so attractive, as was the fascinating world that he'd formed around himself—was so taken by the house, a tangible realisation of his own dreams, that he settled down to stay, brimming with emotion.

_____

"Under the guidance of a highly talented Greek architect" (Claud writes, transparently veiling Paul's identity), Bertie's artistic education began: a process involving the cultural and aesthetic refinement of his very existence.

Although Paul never asked questions—as if everything were implicit—he gradually learnt the details of Bertie's earlier life, which in fact he had guessed from the very first moment.

Bertie was also of Jewish origin and his family had been "Sephardim Jews who, many centuries earlier, had migrated from Mediterranean Africa to Spain and had settled in Toledo. Here they had risen to positions of authority and became *Grandes de España,"* as Claud wrote, not hesitating to note that "since then the family had preserved its aristocratic traditions and excelled in culture, science and religion." Having emigrated to Germany after the Jewish expulsion from Spain, the family had taken the name of the small town near Ulm where they settled: Landsberg, to be precise.

"Bertie's father," reports Claud, "a handsome man of exceptional physical strength, had enrolled as a young man in a highly exclusive German lancer regiment, the Uhlans." Then, when he understood the political direction in which the Empire was moving under Wilhelm I, he decided to leave Germany. The family moved to Brazil where, thanks to his skill in the world of finance, Bertie's father not only "made the family fortune and acquired vast estates" (these are still Claud's words), but won the trust of the Emperor to whom he had promptly offered his services. Bertie was born in Rio de Janeiro on October 12, 1889.

This was the year when Emperor Pedro II of Brazil had finally succumbed to the crisis that would shortly lead to the establishment of the Brazilian Republic: an authoritarian regime based on the support of the colonels. The social tensions that followed this political upheaval were sufficient to persuade "Landsberg" (Claud refers to him throughout solely by his surname, as if he never had a personal identity) to leave Brazil with his family and move to London; this move was also designed to fulfill the wishes of Bertie's mother Lucy Williams, "a singer from a well-known New England family," who was determined to give her children a strictly Anglo-Saxon education. Arriving in London, "with the family, which now included three sons and two daughters, and a full complement of governesses, maids, etc.," Bertie's parents settled "in a handsome house in Lancaster Gate, on the northern edge of Hyde Park, a neighborhood that was particularly popular with rich foreigners."

From a young age, Bertie attended the best private schools in London, beginning at Worthing ("where he underwent strange religious experiences"), and then at Letchworth Garden City and other establishments.

His later education "followed in the steps of Lord Byron." He attended Harrow before going up to Cambridge where he spent four years at Trinity Hall.

In short, Bertie's youth consisted of a sequence of events that were not all that dissimilar to those of Paul Rodocanachi's life some twenty years earlier. It was these events that prompted him, after a series of academic failures at Trinity Hall, to leave London and, like Paul, move to Paris.

Once again, Claud provides a clue—even if the details are slightly inaccurate—to an aspect of Bertie's cultural formation that might otherwise elude us: his almost wholehearted support for the teachings of Henri-Louis Bergson. Where else, if not from the work of the master of French *nouvelle philosophie*, could Bertie have drawn the conviction, which seemed to inspire his whole life, that intuition and aesthetics are two breadly conciding aspects of life?[6]

Moreover, the lectures Bergson gave in Paris during this period were in part social events that in many ways had much in common with the fashionable custom for gentlemen to take morning rides in the Bois de Boulogne.

Fate seemed thus to have led Bertie to a house, such as that in Rue du Centre, which fascinated him; he was attracted by the beauty of its garden that ran along the bank of the Seine, by the composition of its façades, by the harmonious proportion of its rooms, and by the wonderful and beautifully arranged objects that furnished them.

However it was not just this world, so rich in possibilities yet at the same time so intimate, that Bertie grew to know in Paul's company. He also came into contact, from the outset, with a friend of Paul's who was an almost permanent member of the household whenever he visited Paris: a composer, aged a little over thirty, who, despite the signs of the disorder that was already starting to trouble him, was enjoying a period of great success.

Roger Quilter was born in Sussex in 1877; he was also the son of a wealthy businessman, and had been brought up in an environment similar to that which both Paul and Bertie had experienced during their youth in England. But while Bertie had been enriched by his acquaintance with France, Roger's principal influence came from central Europe. Seeking

Paul Rodocanachi, *Portrait of Bertie Landsberg*, 1912

to perfect his musical technique Quilter had enrolled in the
conservatoire at Frankfurt am Main in 1896, where, under the
guidance of excellent German teachers, he had discovered
a special talent for composing songs.[7]

The bond between Paul and this composer reveals the
extent to which Paul felt at home in these circles, which
revolved around the world of entertainment, and how he was
attuned—and in his own way shared—the frenetic social life
that accompanied that particular sphere, especially the theater,
which existed in an almost permanent state of excitement.

———

It was this world that immediately understood the genius
Serge Diaghilev, former manager of the Imperial Theaters
of St Petersburg, as soon as he arrived at the Salon d'Automne
in Paris. It was this same world that praised the first Russian
concert series performed at the Opéra the following year; and
soon after it was completely taken by Diaghilev's most extraordinary invention: *Les Ballets Russes*.

Les Ballets Russes was such a success that when the
plans for a magnificent event, which Diaghilev was organizing
in Paris in 1909, ran into difficulties following the sudden
death of Grand Duke Vladimir, the Tsar's uncle, who had been
its patron, the *grandes dames* of Parisian society came
to his rescue. This group included women of considerable
intelligence and means: not only Countess Greffulhe,
but also "this marvellous creature," who, it was widely believed,
"had been imported in their copious luggage, and as their
most priceless treasure, by the Russian dancers," as Marcel
Proust wrote,[8] introducing under the pseudonym of "Princess
Yourbeletieff" **Misia Sert**, an extraordinary woman whom we
will meet again later in the rooms of La Malcontenta, where Bertie
would subsequently live.

———

Catherine, Baroness d'Erlanger, also hastened to support
Diaghilev. She burst into his changing rooms after a performance just after Paul and Bertie had arrived. She was a woman
of extraordinary charm. Although her figure was now a little
heavier, she had retained, intact, that streak of defiance which
had been amply demonstrated when she attended a high-society
event at Her Majesty's Theatre, London, in 1900 wearing

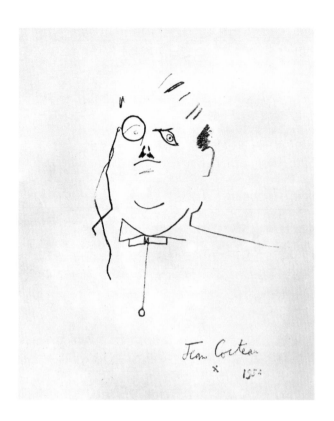

Jean Cocteau, *Serge Diaghilev,* 1954
Pablo Picasso, *Les Ballets Russes,* 1923, program cover
Henri de Toulouse Lautrec, *Misia Godebska* (Madame Natanson at the time,
and later Misia Sert), 1895

a costume designed by Percy Anderson and superbly tailored by B.J. Simmons.[9]

Through the exuberance of her femininity, Catherine displayed all the verve that she had shown as a twenty-one-year-old, when she had first seen Baron Emile d'Erlanger while ice skating in Paris; he was seduced by a display of such vitality, fell deeply in love, and married Catherine in 1895.

Ever aware of artistic matters, Paul barely had time to murmur in Bertie's ear that it was Catherine's father-in-law, Frédéric Emile d'Erlanger who had donated Goya's dramatic "black pictures," painted by the artist in the last years of his life, to the Prado in 1881. Some years later, in 1905, d'Erlanger had also presented the famous series of tapestries based on Raphael's cartoons to the English royal family, in order to furnish Hampton Court.

Paul continued his story as they slowly left the theater. Answering Bertie's questions, Paul told him that Raphael d'Erlanger had received a baronial title—in spite of being of Jewish descent—from the King of Portugal in 1859, for financial services rendered to the Crown, and that the title had later been confirmed by the Austrian Emperor.

Raphael's son, Frédéric Emile, was also a talented busi-nessman. His only mistake had been to back the Confederates in the American Civil War. However, the proceeds from the railway concessions that he had succeeded in obtaining from a prominent senator in Louisiana more than made up for this disaster. Indeed, he had even married the senator's daughter: Emile's mother, and Catherine's mother-in-law.

According to Paul, who continued to instruct his pupil, as a tutor would, Emile did not have the same flair for business as his father and grandfather, but he had made the right decision to leave Paris and move to London. This subsequently became the center of his financial activities during the years of the Dreyfus affair, when France was brimming with dangerously anti-Semitic sentiment. Emile d'Erlanger settled in a magnif-icent house in Hampton Garden. Soon afterwards he bought the property at "One Three Nine Pic" (as Catherine would always call Number 139, Piccadilly), which had previously been Lord Byron's London residence during his brief marriage.

Philip Alexius de László, *Catherine d'Erlanger,* 1899
Oliver Messel, *Catherine d'Erlanger,* 1925
Catherine d'Erlanger, c. 1930

THE HOME OF THE ARTS.
The Wonders of the Baroness d'Erlanger's Town-House in Piccadilly—once the Home of Lord Byron.
By FLORENCE ROBERTS.

IT would seem that the great house at 139 Piccadilly has been specially dedicated to the Arts.

For there, where the poet Byron once made his home, the Baroness d'Erlanger—herself an artist, and an ardent lover of Music and the Drama—has, during the last eight years or so, gathered together such treasure-trove of rare tapestries, and prints, and books, and furnishings, as have made the great place one of the wonder-houses of London, and, indeed, of the world.

So she is carrying on most worthily —and, actually, increasing—its record of fame.

And for some time, too, the Baroness has been putting her artistic talents to very practical and patriotic use, many different war-charity performances having been helped to special success—and profit—by the tableaux and living pictures which she has arranged and rehearsed with infinite care.

Only this last week her record in this way included such complete contrasts, and equal successes, as some delightful Kate Greenaway *tableaux*; a series of Persian pictures; and a succession of Shakespeare, Botticelli, Augustus John, *Chu Chin Chow*, etc.)—these last being a notable feature of the garden-party given at St. James's Palace in aid of the Nation's Fund for Nurses.

Wherefore it will be gathered that her artistic tastes are varied and far extending.

THE FASHIONS OF YESTERDAY—

Her preference for one period is, however, suggested, by a collection of gowns and all sorts of early Victorian dress details, and it was, of course, from this wonderful store that the dressing of the Kate Greenaway *tableaux* was so successfully achieved.

Some of the lovely silken things were still displayed at the end of the great drawing-room when I called, and the Baroness pulled open the drawers of one or two veritable treasure-chests, and showed them full of other silken survivals of bygone days, and fashions.

She took out one—a dress whose silk was of the hue of old parchment, and hand-painted with very-fading had lent a new charm of softness to colourings which were all repeated in the lattice-lacing of ribbons on the bodice—and held it up for my admiration.

AND THE FASCINATION OF TO-DAY.

But to me there was infinitely more attraction in the fashions of to-day, as most fascinatingly represented by her own soft, simple, and most graceful gown of grey *charmeuse*, with a deep silken broidery bordering the loosely-girdled tunic corsage.

Grey, too, were silken stockings and *suède* shoes, and set on the bright beautiful hair was a little grey toque all encircled with fairly laid, lightly-curled ostrich feathers. Pearls hung round her neck, a white fox-skin was slung about her shoulders, and just one great emerald struck a

dominant note of glorious colour in this minor chord of delicate shadings.

So I proclaimed my preference for the fashions of to-day rather than of yesterday, and "Don't

THE BARONESS D'ERLANGER, WHOSE TOWN HOUSE AT 139 PICCADILLY WAS ONCE THE HOME OF LORD BYRON.

IN THE BOUDOIR OF THE BARONESS JADE GREEN AND GOLD TOGETHER MAKE A PERFECT COLOUR-FRAME FOR A THOUSAND AND ONE THINGS OF BEAUTY.

you think that dress is almost perfect now? I queried—so comfortable and graceful."

But while admitting all this, the Baroness laughingly refused to forswear her already proclaimed devotion to the old-world styles, and picturesqueness.

There was another point, too—concerning her Convalescent Home at Shooter's Hill—on which I had wanted to collect some information.

But, as regards her own doings, she was firmly uncommunicative, though her house, she placed at the disposal —and the mercy—of my pen.

I did gather, however, that, for some time at the beginning of the war, this same Home was transformed into a hospital for soldiers, many of the Belgian wounded being accommodated there. But eventually, and because of its nearness to the great Military Hospital at Woolwich, the Baroness found its help was not so urgently needed, and therefore closed it for the time being.

THE FIRST CRÈCHE FOR THE BABIES OF LONDON.

Its original purpose, though, was to benefit the babies, in whose welfare she has always taken the keenest interest.

In fact, and working in conjunction with Muriel Lady Helmsley, she founded, some eighteen years ago, what was, she thinks, the very first—and certainly the second—of the now numerous *crèches*, whose benefits are so universally recognised.

So, naturally, she took the keenest interest in Baby Welfare Week, seeing that it represented the development of one of her own special interests, and increasing the arrangements for a Pound Day at Hoxton being another of the many varied occupations of that one well-filled week, which is, indeed, typical of any number of others.

So that, just at present, she does not see much of that beautiful home of hers.

SOMETHING OF A PALACE—AND, STILL, EVERYTHING OF A HOME.

It is a palatial place, with its marble entrance hall and stairs—and its drawing-room, supposed to be the largest in London, which opens, at one end, into the famous Chinese room, and at the other into the boudoir.

But, with all its splendour, it still manages to be a veritable, and delightful, home.

And everywhere there is evidence of its beautiful owner's artistic tastes—rough tracings and finished sketches, suggestions for figure groupings, and landscape backgrounds for *tableaux*; while upstairs, and next to the big bedroom, is a painting-room, where the walls are covered with drawings and pictures of every kind, a cover from a magazine, having a place of honour next to a finished and framed picture—a recognition being, indeed, given to beauty of colour and form, wherever it may be found.

The big central table is covered with palettes and paint-boxes, but, still, this is not the real work-room where the Baroness painted her latest picture which is now hung in the Grosvenor Gallery.

C

Catherine d'Erlanger dressed for the ball at Her Majesty's Theatre,
London, 1900 (photo: The Lafayette Studio)

Catherine fulfilled her marital duties just as impetuously as she tackled life: within as many years, she and Emile had had four children. After this their marriage settled into an agreement that allowed Emile to surround himself with people who flattered his ambitions to become an amateur poet, while Catherine— bolstered by a temperament that knew no hesitation—threw her- self into a vortex of new friends and acquaintances, exciting experiences and society events, through which she gained an increasing degree of freedom.

The handsome house, which had been Byron's, became the epicenter of the exuberant lifestyle of "Marie Rose Antoinette Catherine d'Aqueria de Capellis de Rochegude," as Claud liked to call this proud but dynamic woman, thus emphasizing her noble birth as well as her multifaceted personality.

The house became the meeting place for intellectuals and aristocrats, as well as young artists in search of success.[10] Among the latter were **Philip Alexius De László**[11] and also a young French diplomat, **Paul Morand**, who frenetically moved from one aristocratic circle to the next in all the Euro- pean capitals. Paul was captivated by Catherine's charm and wrote a memorable account of her, disguising her true identity under the pseudonym *Clarisse*.

———

"We used to meet every night in the best-lit and most sonorous houses in town, where we would dance," he wrote in 1914.[12]

In portraying Catherine, Morand proceeds in fits and starts, as if following sudden intuitions. He praises her stature, the breadth of her shoulders, her constitution, the color of her hair (and the satisfaction she derived from displaying her spectacular hairstyles), the mystery of her lips, the sensuality of her nose with its restless nostrils, and the attractiveness of her yellow eyes. He evokes her sparkling health, the beat of her pulse, the physical and mental joy with which she moved. In short, he contemplates her body from all angles, and every aspect of her behavior, as if the sum were a single work of art, a symphony of almost unattainable aesthetic perfection.

"Without being well-educated, you know a great deal. You know nothing of history, but you know the past and you understand it better than a scholar when you hold a piece

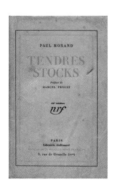

Paul Morand (photo: Berenice Abbott)
Paul Morand, *Tendres Stocks*, Paris 1929, front cover and title page with dedication
by Paul Morand to Bertie Landsberg, 1957, and by Claud Phillimore to Antonio Foscari
(Tonci), 1981

of embroidery, or an old slipper, in your hands. You do not like books. I have never seen you read a novel. In your library there are only pictures, documents and catalogues."[13]

In another passage, still inspired by Catherine's physical presence, Morand writes: "All day, she roams around the suburban antique dealers, the second-hand shops of the Hebrew districts, the clothes vendors. Basket in hand, she sets off, with her long strides, to the scrap merchants and, unconcerned about fleas, approaches the dealers, rummages around with her rag-and-bone man's instinct and returns home, her pockets and muff laden with new trinkets. She accommodates them all, from the rarest object to screws, doorknobs, nails, old coins."[14]

Writing the introduction to *Tendres Stocks,* a collection of Morand's short stories that included this description of Catherine, previously published in *Le Mercure de France*, Marcel Proust was right to point out that Morand, with this rapid succession of images, revealed a certain inability to grasp, and therefore to define, the personality of this woman who "has more sparkle than the women, more self-assurance than the men." Yet it was precisely this difficulty in focusing on an elusive, hard-to-define figure that provides the most effective demonstration of the immediacy with which this extraordinary creature managed to evade a man's acquaintance with instinctive ease.

Proust's criticism of Paul Morand is, to some extent, similar to the criticism of Catherine made by a *grande dame* of the period who was only a few years older. Like Catherine, she spoke perfect English, was intimately acquainted with Bergson whose lectures she had attended at the Collège de France, and kept an open house for the intellectuals and artists she liked.

Elisabeth de Gramont—who was married at a very young age to the Marquis (and later Duke) of Clermont-Tonnerre—also stood out for her aristocratic *allure*, which she used unashamedly to her advantage. Unlike Catherine, however, Elisabeth held firm political opinions, usually Marxist, and her inexhaustible energy allowed her to express her views and to take an active part in events from which Catherine was objectively excluded. Moreover, having announced her homosexuality, Elizabeth used this, too, to express her identity, without any trace of bourgeois prudence.

A Misunderstood Masterpiece

Just as Marcel Proust viewed Paul Morand as a person
(and a writer) who was distracted by superficial observations,
Gramont thought that Catherine's behavior was individualistic
and self-referential, in spite of its defiance. It was as if something restrained the Baroness from discovering her identity and
from openly and truthfully declaring her character—as if the
reference framework for her existence was the social grouping
to which she herself belonged, rather than to a new, and
real entity: namely that "audience" which, for the Duchess,
was a natural point of reference and in front of whom she had
absolutely no hesitation in displaying her own individuality.

The differences between the two women—which seem
to throw light on each other's personality—are clearly evident
if we focus on the relationships both sought to cultivate
with art and artists.

Elizabeth dedicated herself to writing every day, building
up a memorable correspondence in which she recorded her
love affairs, almost as though to turn her sentimental life into a
work of art. Catherine, on the other hand, spent time painting,
but did so without creating any sense of order in her artistic
output, without documenting it. She limited herself almost exclusively to portraits, which allowed her to establish a personal
relationship with her sitters: indeed, by posing in front of her,
her subjects offered her a glimpse into their individual world.[15]

_____

Perhaps it was by following Catherine—or merely by following
the course of that river, in which she was like a foaming
wave—that Bertie also started to frequent the artists' circles
and avant-garde galleries that were so in vogue in Paris
at that time. He was certainly able to meet and get to know
Georges Braque, **Pablo Picasso**, and **Henri Matisse**,
developing friendships that would last for years. For example,
he became a genuine admirer of Matisse. He even managed
to persuade his father, "the" Landsberg, to commission
a portrait of his sister Yvonne, who had followed him to Paris.

One of the drawings done by Matisse as a study of this
young woman—who, to be honest, was not very attractive—
would be kept by Bertie for some time, not least as a way of
remembering the singular outcome of the story. When Matisse
showed Yvonne her portrait, she burst into tears; horror-struck,

she refused to accept it. Matisse was kind enough to try
and console the poor young woman, but later sold the fabulous
painting, which is now proudly owned by the Philadelphia
Museum of Art and which represents one of the principal masterpieces of its collections.[16]

This episode, like Catherine's portrait that was penned
at around the same time by Morand, dates from 1914,
the year when the war that would alter Europe's destiny
broke out.

These historical events were so dramatic that Catherine,
with her apolitical mentality, found them completely incomprehensible. While the Duchesse de Gramont went to inspect
the frontline and work in a military hospital, Catherine stayed
in London and kept as far as possible from the tragedies on the
continent. Surrounded by water, as Morand noted, she felt
protected.

Rodocanachi, who kept his British citizenship, remained
in his house in Rue du Centre, perhaps with Quilter who
was unable to enlist due to the heart problems that undermined
his state of health. As a Brazilian citizen, Bertie probably
returned to Brazil.[17]

During these years, from 1914 to 1917, Bertie—whether
or not he was actually in Brazil—wrote about forty poems, which
were subsequently published in what Claud called "a slim
volume of sensitive poems."

———

Re-reading them today, the poems reveal how Bertie's
education was up-to-date in literary terms, yet suffered from
a Victorian cultural conditioning which he would never cast off
for the rest of his life. The erotic content, at the heart of these
compositions, is not freely expressed; it remains veiled by
naturalistic metaphors, at times almost transparent. At this stage
of Bertie's life, his homosexuality was sublimated in the search
for life and beauty, and was seen ideally as the choice of a
way of life.

It may have been through Catherine's influence that,
in 1922, these compositions were printed by Elkin Matthews
(a publisher attentive to contemporary English literature,
and who had published Ezra Pound's works since 1909) in a
book whose title, *Tumult and Order*, clearly expresses Bertie's

Henri Matisse, *Mademoiselle Yvonne Landsberg,* painting and preparatory drawing,
both 1914

BRUCE CHATWIN

L.6. (top) Albany

London W.I.

4th October 1979

Dear Antonio,

A small contribution to the library of Malcontenta.
I have never seen another copy other than the one Bertie gave
me. Also a photo of the drawing of Mlle Landsberg: the other
one that Bertie sold is both finer and uglier and is now
in the Museum of Modern Art, New York.

I seem to be having difficultues getting the
neo-classical chair copied. Is there a craftsman is your
area who could copy just <u>one</u> of yours, so I can use it as a
model? Absolutely no hurry, because we have'nt moved house
yet.

It was wonderful, and for me very moving, to see
the house again - and in such hands as yours!

amicalement,

Bruce Chatwin

Bruce Chatwin, letter to Antonio Foscari, October 4, 1979

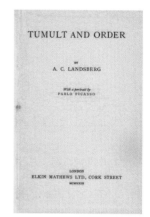

TUMULT AND ORDER

BY
A. C. LANDSBERG

With a portrait by
PABLO PICASSO

LONDON
ELKIN MATHEWS LTD, CORK STREET
MCMXXIII

SPRING

Summer, when thick leaves wink
In the sun, and white clouds roll,
    stately, in the sky;
Autumn, when great pears droop
And leaves die braving threatening skies
    with red and gold;
Winter, whose roughest winds
Cannot awake the earth richly sleeping
    beneath the snow;

Seem all but preparation,
Or else the true vibration,
Of Spring when all things grow,
Swelling with joy like flow
Of a great melody;

A dancer who cannot err,
A race-horse needing no spur,
Foam on the crest of a wave,
Strength which death itself can brave,
Such is the glorious Spring!

"Spring," from Bertie Landsberg,
        Tumult and Order

Pablo Picasso, *Bertie Landsberg*, 1922
Bertie Landsberg, *Tumult and Order*, London 1923, front cover and dedication

aspiration to bring order, through his writing, to the turmoil of emotions jostling for space in his soul.

One need only note that Bertie dedicated the booklet to Paul Rodocanachi and Roger Quilter (as well as to his mother, who remained firmly at his side) to realize that the house in Rue du Centre was still, after the War, the fulcrum of his life. Moreover, the inclusion on the first page of his portrait by Picasso, painted in 1922, was proof of the fact that cultural and social life in Paris resumed almost immediately at the end of the First World War.

That portrait (donated by Claud Phillimore to the Fitzwilliam Museum in Cambridge) is enlightening because, with Picasso's characteristic incisiveness, it shows how Bertie learned to temper the natural elegance of his bearing with the accepted norms of composure which had the same effect in his relations with others as that sense of inner order he had tried to achieve through writing.

————

This small volume of Bertie's poems was published just before Catherine's favorite daughter, **Liliane Marie Mathilde** (Baba), was married with much ado in Westminster Cathedral on November 14, 1923.

It was an event that, to some extent, helped to set Catherine even further apart from her husband's family, prompting her gradual withdrawal from London. The reason for this was that, against her husband's wishes, Catherine had encouraged Baba's marriage to a brilliant young nobleman, **Prince Jean-Louis of Faucigny-Lucinge**, who was not yet twenty years old. The young couple's house immediately became the most fashionable venue in a city that was, as Faucigny-Lucinge himself admitted, "desperate for fresh blood," and Catherine neither could nor clearly wanted to compete.

Moreover, there were plenty of occasions for Catherine to get away from London. For example, she never would have missed the premiere of a ballet organized by Diaghilev at the Théâtre des Champs Elysées on June 20, 1924. It would not have mattered to her at all that many more conventional theater-goers, who knew the story of **Jean Cocteau**'s play, thought the performance was superficial and frivolous. The

"Baba" d'Erlanger, Princess of Faucigny-Lucinge, 1935

dancers' costumes were designed by **Coco Chanel** and, even more importantly, the backdrop consisted of the huge canvas, *Deux femmes courants sur la plage*, which Picasso had been painting two years earlier when he had portrayed Bertie so eloquently.

The title of the performance, *Le train bleu*, was itself an invitation to depart for the south, to head towards the warmth of the Mediterranean.

_____

Yet the Côte d'Azur was not the destination that Catherine and Bertie (now regularly at her side) had in mind. This was because April 1924 marked an anniversary that, in many respects, would prove highly significant: it was the centenary of **Lord Byron**'s death. This event unleashed the imagination of the passionate lady residing in Piccadilly in the house that had formerly belonged to that romantic adventurer, ardent lover, and poet, whose works she found bewitching. In her excitement, her exuberance would have easily sufficed to affect Paul's young friend; indeed, since boyhood Bertie had decided to lead his life by "following in Byron's steps." The decision to depart for Venice, therefore, became an inescapable reality.

Traveling from Switzerland, Lord Byron had arrived in Venice in 1816, accompanied by servants, horses, monkeys, parrots, and the entire sophisticated armory of objects needed in order to lead a life of constant spectacle, combined with the vigor for which he was renowned. It was in Venice, "that pleasant country" (as he himself would describe it, re-evoking Shakespeare's words), that he wanted to be buried, so that his mortal remains would be united forever with what remained of a civilization, like that enjoyed by Venice in the past, which had absorbed the dazzling rays of the East.

Yet there was also another, very different, reason which prompted Catherine and Bertie to embark on their travels: their vision of the world was such that they could not contemplate life without an elitist and society element.

_____

Venice had witnessed the arrival of a lady whom, according to **Bernard Berenson**, even the Duke of Alba and Prince Beauvais might have considered marrying had she not been divorced; what was more, this lady had started to organize

Coco Chanel and Cecil Beaton (t.l., photo: John Phillips)
Jean Cocteau and Serge Diaghilev (t.r.)
Four performers in *Le train bleu*, music by Darius Milhaud, choreography by
Bronislava Nijinska, plot by Jean Cocteau, costumes by Coco Chanel, premiered by
Diaghilev Ballet Russes, Théâtre des Champs-Elysées, Paris, June 20, 1924 (b.l.)
Pablo Picasso, backdrop for *Le train bleu*, 1924 (b.r.)

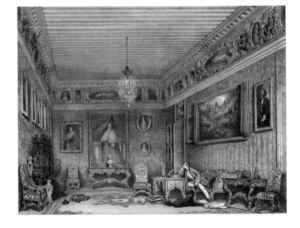

Lord G. Byron, *I due Foscari*, Savona 1845, front cover (t.l.)
Robert Graves, *George Gordon Byron, 6th Baron Byron*, 1836,
line engraving after Thomas Phillips (t.r.)
Giuseppe Verdi, *I due Foscari*, Rome 1844, front cover (b.l.)
Joseph Nash, *Lord Byron in Venice in Palazzo Mocenigo*, 1843, lithograph (b.r.)

a party that would undoubtedly prove memorable. Yet this was not the only reason for Catherine wanting to meet **Linda Lee Thomas**. After leaving her former husband, Edward Russell Thomas, this energetic American woman married **Cole Porter**, a man eight years her junior and a former student at the *Schola Cantorum* directed by Vincent d'Indy. While in Paris, Porter had learned to live in the exclusive pursuit of pleasure ("which is not happiness," as was wittily said even then, "although they look very alike").

Linda's interest in this young man—as her friends knew well—was not motivated by sexual interest, but purely by her vocation as a talent scout. In this, her interest was similar to the instinct that had prompted Catherine to encourage de László a few years earlier. It was a vocation that would lead Linda to further Cecil Beaton's artistic career, and now made her determined to introduce Cole Porter into the most exclusive social circles.

Linda had arrived in Venice a year earlier in the company of Cole Porter, who wore his evening tails with an elegance and sophistication only Yale could teach. Porter had studied there, taking great care not to reveal his social background to anyone, or the extent of the wealth his grandfather, J.O. Cole, had accumulated from the vast coal and oil reserves he had discovered in Sierra Nevada.

Linda was resolute in her efforts to promote and back Cole Porter: she didn't think twice about asking **Igor Stravinsky** to give him composition lessons, or persuading **George Bernard Shaw** to second him in cultural circles, or arranging for Diaghilev to engage him for one of his performances.

In turn Linda was to some extent assisted by an American journalist, whose charm and power lay in her ability to combine, to unique effect, a physical appearance of disconcerting ugliness with a natural flair—one might even say an open-mindedness—that was instantly striking. **Elsa Maxwell** had been engaged by **Giuseppe Volpi**, a very talented entrepreneur, to come to Venice for at least two months every summer, in order to promote high-society life on the beaches in front of the grand hotels he controlled. Volpi was so pleased with Elsa's success that he convinced Mussolini to award her a special medal for her services to Italian tourism.

Linda Lee Thomas, 1926

Gerald Murphy, Jinny Carpenter, Cole Porter, and Sara Murphy in Venice, 1923

Having spent a few months in the evocative rooms of Palazzo Barbaro, almost in symbiosis with **Gerald and Sara Murphy**, Linda moved into another palace in Venice, then owned by the Papadopoli family. It overlooked the Grand Canal and had an imposing façade topped by two large obelisks. It was here, in this impressive building, that she decided to hold a party and, to ensure its social success, asked Diaghilev to oversee its organization. Diaghilev was very much at home in Venice at the time, since he had visited the city for at least a week's rest every summer for years, almost always accompanied by **Nijinsky**.

Catherine knew this and she also knew that this particular year, in Nijinsky's absence, Diaghilev had invited **Serge Lifar** to stay. It was enough to spur her into action, responding to an impulse that prevented her from realizing how severely Italian public opinion had been shaken over the summer by an event with sinister overtones and a dramatic outcome: the kidnapping and assassination of a Socialist member of parliament, **Giacomo Matteotti**, who had but recently given a strongly critical speech against the current head of state, **Benito Mussolini**, in the Chamber of Deputies.

When she decided to leave, Catherine—or *Mimì* as she would soon be known—remembered that she had a house in Venice (she called it a *palazzina*, or small palace) overlooking the Rio di San Barnaba, and accessed from the top of Fondamenta Gherardini (at Number 2622). She also took pride in tracing her illustrious ancestors who formed part of the Venetian patriciate. One of the many surnames she bore proudly was Capellis; proof enough to her that she descended from the family of the Venetian noblewoman Bianca Cappello, who had married the Grand Duke of Tuscany, Francesco I de' Medici, in 1579.

It is almost self-evident that, having decided to come to Venice—where she would inevitably be compared to Linda— our Baroness arranged to be accompanied by a man who was as elegant as Cole, and if anything more handsome; Bertie was also younger than Catherine, just as Cole was younger than Linda.

The destination of Catherine's and Bertie's journey was therefore Venice. However, since Bertie only knew Italy and

Cole Porter and Elsa Maxwell at the Lido (t.l.)
Cole Porter's Jazz band at the Lido (t.r.)
Linda Lee Thomas and Noël Coward at the Lido (m.)
Cole Porter, Linda Lee Thomas, Bernard Berenson, and Howard Sturges in gondola (b.l.)
Gerald Murphy in Venice (b.r.)

Cole Porter at the Lido, 1923

The Scampi

Once there lived a nice young Scampi
In a canal that was dark and damp, he
Found his home life much too wet,
And longed to travel with the supper set.
Poor little Scampi.
Fate was kind for very soon a-
Long came the chef from the Hotel Luna,
Saw that Scampi lying there,
And said, "I'll put you on my bill of fare."
Lucky little Scampi.
See him on his silver platter,
Hearing the Queens of the Lido chatter,
Getting the latest in regard
To Elsa Maxwell and Lady Cunard.
Thrilled little Scampi.
See that ambitious Scampi we know
Feeding the Princess San Faustino.
Think of his joy as he gaily glides
Down to the middle of her Roman insides.
Proud little Scampi.
After dinner the Princess Jane
Said to her hostess, "I've such a pain.
"Don't be cross, but I think I shall
"Go for a giro in a side canal."
Scared little Scampi.
Off they went through the troubled tide,
The gondola rocking from side to side.
They tossed about that poor young Scampi
Found that his quarters were much too crampy.
Up comes the Scampi.
Back once more where started from
He said, "I haven't a single qualm,
For I've had a taste of the world, you see,
And a great Princess had a taste of me."
Wise little Scampi.

Cole Porter, *The Scampi* (later *Tale of the Oyster*)

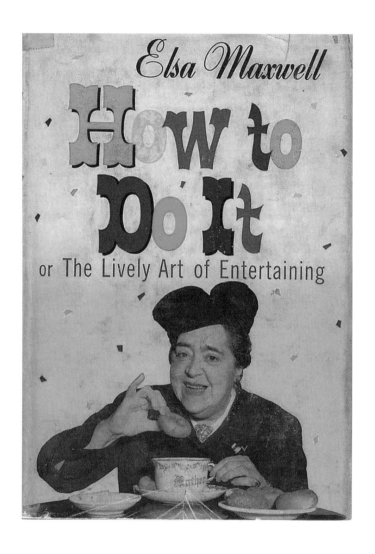

Elsa Maxwell, *How To Do It, or The Lively Art of Entertaining*, Boston 1957, front cover

Elsa Maxwell with a crown and sceptre, 1934 (photo: Cecil Beaton)

its architecture through the books that filled Paul's bookshelves in Paris, it was inevitable that this Italian tour, however brief, should start from the city that gave new birth to the burgeoning spring of the spirit which—not long before—had been evocatively called the "Renaissance."

But their visit in Florence was not long. On leaving Tuscany, Catherine and Bertie visited Ravenna and Mantua, but only fleetingly because they were keen to reach Padua and, from there, to continue towards the lagoons surrounding *La Serenissima*, the very city that Byron had chosen, at an exciting period in his tumultuous life, as the setting for his adventures and where now, with Diaghilev's help, Linda and Cole Porter were rediscovering a new theatricality.

The party at Palazzo Papadopoli was due to be held on July 31. By a stroke of good fortune the evening took place after a sudden thunderstorm had unleashed a deluge on the city, spreading panic throughout the city and sinking several gondolas.

From the moment he agreed to organize this event, Diaghilev had dealt with everything with the same authoritarian, almost dictatorial manner he automatically assumed upon entering a theater. A stage was constructed against the side wall of the palace garden, overlooking the Grand Canal. Three arches, decked with climbers, served as the backdrop to the stage. Classical statues, which had been lent by a Venetian museum—without too many questions being asked—were placed under the arches. Powerful spotlights were trained on the key areas. At the preordained time, a procession of sumptuous gondolas drew up in front of the palace, manned by gondoliers in red and gold or red and black liveries. Spectators took up their places in the garden, where colored cushions had been strewn on the ground around a number of carefully placed seats for the guests. In his dance Serge Lifar was partnered by **Lydia Sokolova**, as neither **Alice Nikitina** nor **Tilly Losch** were in Venice at the time. The program consisted of a short *divertissement* in the form of two male variations from *Les Matelots*, followed by *La Tarantella*, *Cimarosiana*, and the dance of the hostess, with her two men, from *Les Biches*.[18]

This was the first and last time that Diaghilev agreed to organize a private party in Venice, partly because he was infuriated by the boldness with which some of the guests, in their enthusiasm, presented gifts to "his" dancers. But perhaps what alarmed him more than anything was the discovery, on hearing Cole Porter play the piano in the palace just as the party was ending, that this American, whom he'd refused to take into consideration, was truly a composer, one who might even be the genius of a new musical genre.

But let us leave this theatrical evening, the glittering presence of international guests, the spectacle of the gondoliers' brightly colored liveries, and indeed Venice itself. Let us go back to Catherine and Bertie and the last phase of their journey.

———

In Padua this striking woman (if for no other reason than for her luxuriant flame-colored hair) and the elegant man who accompanied her visited Giotto's frescos in the chapel that was built for the Scrovegni family but which, once the latter had disappeared, then belonged to the Foscari family for more than three centuries. The two travelers admired the large equestrian statue of a *condottiere* by Donatello, cast in bronze using classical techniques and commissioned by **Francesco Foscari**, the Doge of Venice who secured the greatest expansion of the Repubublic's *stato di terra* (Venice's mainland dominions).

Leaving Padua behind them, our two travelers set out for Venice along the towpath that follows the Riviera del Brenta, the waterway that had linked the two cities for centuries. Having reached Stra, they asked the driver (Bertie never deigned to drive a car) to stop in front of a building whose small pronaos looked towards the Riviera, raised on a high basement.[19] This was the residence where Lord Byron—the male personification of Catherine's defiance, and the poet whose centenary was being celebrated in this fateful year of 1924—retired when Venice exploded with the scandal of his passionate, and above all manifestly public, love affair with a young married woman whom he had met in the circle of intellectuals that gathered in Teotochi Albrizzi's palace.

The sight of this building was emotional for both Catherine and Bertie. Spurred into action, they wasted no time in resuming their journey. Their next stop was the *fabbrica* built by Andrea Palladio for the two brothers, descendants of Doge

Serge Lifar and Serge Diaghilev at the Lido, 1928
Serge Lifar in *Les Matelots*, 1925 (photo: Man Ray)

Léon Voizikovsky, Serge Lifar, Lydia Sokolova, and Serge Diaghilev at the Lido, 1927

Bertie Landsberg

Francesco Foscari, whose personal drama had been retold
by Byron: the Doge had been forced to condemn his own
son to death—the last of eleven—to uphold the strict political
regulations of the Venetian Republic. As they drove East,
Bertie and Catherine, both opera lovers, hummed arias from
Verdi's *I due Foscari*, whose libretto is based on Byron's
account of the tragic affair.

With all these events crowding their minds, they almost
missed the sumptuous sight of Villa Pisani (reserved at the time
for the use of Italy's royal family); they did not even contemplate stopping to admire Tiepolo's frescos in the main salon, or
to visit the maze, which is one of the main attractions of its vast
garden. They didn't notice the heavy barges slowly gliding
down the waters of the Riviera carrying sand, bricks, and demi-
johns filled with wine to Venice nor the linen for those hotels
whose laundries were in the Venetian hinterland. Nor did
they notice the brackish smell that grows more intense as one
approaches the *conterminazione*, namely the official boundary
of the Republic, which separates the *terraferma* from the
lagoons.

Rounding yet another bend in the river, they suddenly
saw, partly covered by the leafy branches of a single poplar,
the *palazzo* built by Andrea Palladio for the two magnificent
Foscari brothers, **Nicolò** and **Alvise**.[20]

A few minutes later, the *fabbrica* (as Palladio himself tended
to call the villa) appeared in front of them. It stood solemn
and beautiful, showing that neither time nor neglect can undermine the purity of theoretical design when expressed in the
rigorous language of a man—in this case, an architect—who
has fully reached his cultural maturity.

A message of this kind is so rare that it elicits a profoundly
emotional response in the viewer and generates a sense
of unutterable intellectual enjoyment in anyone who can understand its full meaning.

"It is a house built for human habitation, using elements
of divine architecture," wrote **George Matei Cantacuzino**,
an aristocrat educated at the École des Beaux-Arts in Paris,
who visited Bertie and stayed in this *palazzo* on more than
one occasion. "Overlooking a scene of great desolation ... the

sole vertical element on these ancient marshes from which the sea has withdrawn, this simple cubic house, fronted by a colonnaded loggia and a pediment with magnificent stairs with inverted balustrades and gaping windows, creates an extraordinary impression on the passer-by, as it rises out of the morning mist or fades in the dusk."

Cantacuzino continues: "The effects of time seems to have worked in full accord with the architecture: time has obliterated almost all the ornamentation, laying the brick bare, simplifying the mouldings, and reducing the building to nothing but a simple play of volumes, its austere outline reflected in a disused canal. Standing in front of this derelict building, one can meditate at length on the secrets of success achieved with such ease ... like all victories of various forms."[21]

Our travelers, still reeling from the impact of an emotion that had affected all their senses, were brought back to the present by the noise of a passing tram, that strange electrified vehicle that used to run along the road, opposite the waterway. No watch could have gauged the time that passed before they decided to take a few steps, looking for a way to cross the Riviera which made the Palladian *fabbrica* (villa) look like a mirage, floating on the other side of the water.

They had to wait for a bridge-keeper, wielding a large rusty handle, to finish closing a swing bridge that had just been opened to let a vessel pass.[22] They drove the last stretch of road in silence, respectful of the place's sacredness and in order not to profane the aura of solitude that permeated it. They pushed open a gate, which was only half-closed, and discovered another façade, different from the one they had just admired. It was skillfully composed, but still mysterious. No one came out to greet them. Slowly they pushed the main entrance door open.

Silence pervaded the ground-floor rooms; the robust vaulted ceilings only augmented the feeling that this was more of an initiation than a visit. They climbed a chipped spiral staircase. Neither the traces of the recent military occupation[23] nor the smell of grain, which was once more being stored in the building after the war, could distract their attention, which was focused—with almost agonizing tension—on the purity of the spaces conceived by Andrea Palladio. The perfection of his

architecture was exalted by the whiteness of the walls:
a diffused glimmer from which the remnants of a fresco cycle
emerged, in part covered by a dull coat of whitewash. Nothing
had broken or even disturbed the harmony that had reigned
here for centuries.

It does not take long to drive from Malcontenta to Fusina.
The towpath from Padua ends here on the banks of the lagoon.
Bertie and Catherine climbed into a gondola, almost without
exchanging a word.

In the time that it took them to cross the lagoon, the idea
of the party, which would be held in Palazzo Papadopoli in a
few days' time, had lost much of its former significance. While
waiting to meet Paul (who had decided to travel to Venice
by wagon-lit to avoid the effort of a tour, which seemed a little
too strenuous for his taste), they organized their days in a
way designed extend the exaltation that now filled their minds.

They visited San Francesco della Vigna to admire the
Palladian façade, San Giorgio and its cloisters, and the splendor
of the Redentore. They hastened to see the effigy of Francesco
Foscari which stood above the triumphal doorway leading
into the Doge's Palace, the "large house" which this resolute
leader had built to impose his memory on the Venetian
cityscape, and his tomb, decorated with figures carved by the
best artist employed in Donatello's workshop.

———

When Paul, Catherine and Bertie finally reunited in the *palazzina*
at San Barnaba, they were united by that harmonious sense
of purpose that brings together people who agree to act on
all the aesthetic opportunities and emotions that life has to
offer. It was as if this meeting triggered an alchemical reaction
through which each element was welded to the other to
produce a union of unprecedented strength. Their reciprocal
roles were soon clarified and moulded into a project.

Young Bertie—the member of the trio endowed with
beauty and elegance—was invested with the vitality and culture
that, separately, both Catherine and Paul possessed. He
therefore became the linchpin in this three-part union; moreover,
without a moment's hesitation, he also played the role of
the angel: entrusted with realizing a dream that his partners
could not have pursued alone.

La Malcontenta, east façade, 1925 (photo: Osvaldo Boehm)

La Malcontenta, north façade, 1926 (photo: Osvaldo Boehm)

Catherine found not only in Paul and Bertie but also in this project the human context into which she could pour her exuberantly feminine energy: one that combined a protective urge with organizational skill. In this way—in this abstract "family" that began to emerge—she also found the freedom to express, and to some extent also to exalt, her vocation.

Paul—who didn't want to lose his pupil nor forgo the vital impulse which Catherine offered—found in this Renaissance building of such excellence the beauty and tangible qualities of the past that he'd always tried to evoke in that unique search for quality, which had driven him to build and decorate the house in Rue du Centre.

The strength of this trio therefore rested both on the intellectual complicity that, for some time now, had united all three members, as well as on a series of life choices, which were surprisingly harmonious.

———

In a state of anxiety, which at times exploded into a form of visceral fear, negotiations were started with the owner of this superb architectural monument that had appeared, as if by miracle, on the banks of the Brenta Riviera. The owner, **Lionello Hierschel de Minerbi**, was a man of the world who knew his way in the property sector. In addition to Palazzo Grimani in Santa Maria Formosa, where he worked as an antiquarian, he also owned Ca'Rezzonico in Venice and was angling to rent it—at exactly the same period—to the Porters who were looking for a place that would provide an even more sumptuous residence than Palazzo Papadopoli.

The difficulties that prevented the trio from reaching an agreement with the owner can be attributed to external circumstances. Firstly, Hierschel de Minerbi wanted to sell all the land he owned around the Palladian *fabbrica* (which was all that was left of the estates that had once belonged to the Foscari family). In the second place, Bertie did not have the means to buy such a large property, and indeed he did not even have enough to buy the *palazzo* and its immediate environs.

An Instant Conversion

Bertie had no other choice but to leave immediately for Brazil, hoping to obtain the money from his father, at least in the form of a loan. However, in order to secure a loan, he was finally obliged to approach a local banker upon returning to Venice, and before he could finally buy the property he would also need Catherine's financial support (as Jean-Louis of Faucigny-Lucinge, her son-in-law, indicated over sixty years later, when he wrote his life story).[24]

As soon as the terms of the contract were finalized, on April 1, 1925, Bertie went to La Malcontenta. On reaching the land gate, which stood half-open as always, Catherine and Paul stood back so that Bertie could experience the surge of emotion as he walked into the *palazzo* for the first time as owner.

———

As a result, Bertie, whose emotions were so spontaneous, saw the residence in a new light. As happens in every true conversion, his mind was instantly filled with a series of convictions that perhaps he had never even imagined he might have.

The equipment and things which had been left on the ground floor, and even the furniture and old paintings which Hierschel de Minerbi had left on the *piano nobile* (first floor), were, in Bertie's eyes, completely alien and had to be removed immediately in order to restore the rooms to a condition in which they could accommodate another way of life and other loves: in short, another story. For Bertie, the most pressing requirement was to "liberate" these harmonious spaces from all that filled them.

This feeling—which at the time resulted in almost frenetic activity—led to one of Bertie's most lasting convictions. He discovered that, as each object was removed from the ground floor, and as each chair or piece of furniture, or each painting, was removed from the *piano nobile*, these spaces acquired greater purity and perfection. In other words, he discovered that the most relevant way of exalting the quality of Palladian architecture was to subtract everything that might interfere with the abstract rigor of the proportions the architect had assigned to each space.

At the time Bertie didn't share his conviction with Catherine and Paul, perhaps because he was not yet fully conscious of it himself. But based on this early experience and on the emotion that filled his soul, he decided not to allow Paul to carry out any reinvention of the past or re-elaboration of classical forms, however sophisticated. Nor would he allow Catherine to fill these rooms with the trinkets, shells, ornaments, and other mysterious objects of the kind that fascinated her when she found them in bric-a-brac shops or flea markets, where she inevitably always picked up something for a song.

———

Emptiness—seen as an alternative to any form of furnishings— was what Bertie deliberately intended to maintain, wherever possible, within these walls.

This was the approach used by Bertie when restoring the *fabbrica*—which is all the more surprising when one realizes that it represented a philosophy diametrically opposed to that adopted by Linda and Cole Porter at Ca'Rezzonico where, as soon as they moved in, they hastened to give a party that would be famous for its ostentation and opulence.

Bertie carefully avoided introducing any innovation and allowed only essential work to be carried out: repairs to the roof, the replacement of the chipped steps of the small internal staircase, and the fitting of new ironmongery to the doors and windows which had to look exactly like the existing ones.

It was this timeless interior that Bertie showed his first guests when he opened the doors, less than five months after signing the contract (the time to connect to the water supply and repair the holes in the floors) of the *palazzo* which was by now his home.[25]

In this short space of time, he had also become convinced that the seeming dereliction of the *fabbrica* evoked the "excitement of discovery" in his guests' minds, a sensation that was not dissimilar to what he himself had felt; as it helped communicating the sense of the adventure on which he had embarked by moving into these rooms with Catherine and Paul.

———

These early months—and the surprise, emotions, and enthu- siasm expressed by the visitors who entered these spaces—

were decisive in forming in Bertie's mind a concept that
was just as important as that of respecting the integrity of
the building, in the form in which it had miraculously survived
into the twentieth century. He realized that, in some form
or other, it was fundamental to make this cultural heritage
accessible, both the building and his own conservation theory,
to those who could understand its beauty and perfection.
Therefore the guest—the minimal unit of a public that was virtually infinite—started to become a figure that ideally was present
within the walls of this house.

The guest was not only summoned to provide
a source of constant admiration for such excellent spaces,
understood as a due tribute to beauty. But the existence
of the guest and his or her ideal presence was the almost
inescapable premise for a choice—like the lifestyle chosen
spontaneously by Bertie, Catherine and Paul—that tended
to find expression, perhaps above all, through social events.
The trio's cohesion would soon have faltered, had not the
complicity firmly linking these three lives been put to the test,
day after day, by observers challenged to decipher its enigmas
and implications.

Guests who entered these spaces with their social bag-
gage, their characters, and their behavior, put on performances—
often unconscious—that became all the more pertinent the
more eccentric their individuality, and the more outrageous,
or simply extravagant, the knowledge they brought with
them on either side—those who lived in the house and those
who were invited—staged performances that were constantly
different, switching roles and improvising relationships
and love affairs, programs and events.

What happened at La Malcontenta was thus different
to what happened in the house on Piccadilly in London, or
in the house in Neuilly-sur-Seine. No salon was formed here:
no cycle of people with similar cultural interests, nor were
there any performances like those which Paul used to organize
in his dining-room, in the music room, or in the bedroom or
that special room which he'd built so he could enjoy the sight
and company of dancers invited to display the elegance of
their movements. Instead, in this evocative architectural setting,
Bertie, Catherine, and Paul, with a sense of harmony that

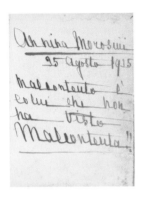

Annina Morosini's signature in the visitors' book, August 1925
Lino Selvatico, *Annina Morosini,* 1910

became more refined with each passing month, interpreted
different characters in a succession of small events.

———

To keep the memory of a "season" rich in such subtle promise,
Catherine gave Bertie—who, with the glorious bearing of
his thirty-five years, was the symbol as well as the protagonist
of this adventure—a book to be signed by all the visitors
whom he welcomed as the owner of the house.

The first signature in the book was that of **Countess
Annina Morosini**, whose fascination is evoked by the description penned by **Lino Selvatico** before the war, when Emperor
Wilhelm II visited her in Venice, nonchalantly wearing a Hussar
jacket over his shoulders to disguise the fact that his left
arm was wasted.[26]

With the passing years, the beautiful Annina became
the emblem of an aristocracy that, wherever possible, avoided
the Lido and the grand hotels overlooking the beach where
a crush of high society revolved around **Princess of San
Faustino**. The latter was a lady of excellent character who
over time had lost none of the freshness and the practicality
of her American education, adding to these an aristocratic
character and demeanor through her marriage. Moreover,
through her daughter Virginia's union to Edoardo Agnelli, she
now held a supremely important place
in the world of Italian industry.

———

Bearing this in mind, it is not hard to understand why the Lido
beaches and the salons of the Excelsior were not, nor could be,
a setting where Bertie, Catherine and Paul could best perform
their self-appointed roles as an "acting company."

For example, Bertie would never, under any circumstances,
have undressed to bathe. However, his reasons for this were
different to Diaghilev's, who similarly had never appeared
in a swimming costume. Bertie did not wish anyone to see that
his body was covered in tattoos, from top to toe. For a clearer
understanding of the reasons that prevented him from frequent-
ing the Lido it is worth remembering that Diaghilev, who for
years had stayed at the Excelsior, decided to leave this hotel,
so much the heart of society life, at precisely this time because
he was annoyed by the "unbearable racket." The truth was that,

DE GAUCHE À DROITE :
LE PRINCE J.-L. DE FAUCI-
GNY-LUCINGE, LA PRIN-
CESSE CITO-FILOMARINO
DI BITTETO, LA COMTES-
SE A. DE ROBILANT, LE
MARQUIS SALINA AMORI-
NI, LA PRINCESSE J.-L. DE
FAUCIGNY-LUCINGE ET M.
CHARLES DE BESTEIGUI

Prince and Princess of Faucigny-Lucinge, Charles de Beistegui,
and others, 1930 (from Catherine d'Erlanger's scrapbook)
Jane Campbell, Princess of San Faustino at the Lido, August 1932
Catherine d'Erlanger, Jane Campbell, Princess of San Faustino,
and friends at the Lido, August 1932 (photos b.l. and b.r.: Cecil Beaton)

DRAWING LOTS FOR MODELS —
Numbers of artists spent their time painting on the famous beach.
Models were drawn for by lot, and included Lady Bridget Parsons, Princesse Jane de

Faustino and Miss Tilly Losch. Those who shared them included Lady Diana Abdy—who executed a very good portrait of Lady Bridget —the Baroness d'Erlanger, Mr. Cecil Beaton, Mr. Oliver Messel, and Mrs. von Reppert Bismarck.
Mrs. Bismarck, you remember, held an exhibition of her work in London not long ago.

Catherine d'Erlanger, Cecil Beaton, and Tilly Losch at the Lido, August 1932 (photo: Cecil Beaton)
Catherine d'Erlanger, 1931 (photo: Alexander Bassano)
Catherine d'Erlanger at the Lido, 1932 (from Catherine d'Erlanger's scrapbook)

67

Diaghilev continued not to recognize Cole Porter's art, and begancto find Porter's presence on the heterogeneous Venetian scene annoying.

"The whole of Venice," he would soon write to **Boris Kochno,** his lifelong companion as well as his personal assistant, "is up in arms against Cole Porter because of his jazz and his Negroes [the group of musicians and dancers that Linda had hired for him]. He has started an idiotic nightclub on a boat [known as Noah's Ark] moored opposite the Salute, and now the Grand Canal is swarming with the very same Negroes who have made us all run away from London and Paris. They're teaching the Charleston on the Lido beach! It's dreadful! ... The very fact of their [Linda and Cole Porter's] renting Palazzo Rezzonico is considered characteristic of nouveaux riches."[27]

Diaghilev's outburst does, however, reveal his underlying feelings: Kochno, his precious Kochno, had been approached by Linda. It was through her that Kochno met Cole Porter and started "a passionate love affair." This relationship, as well as being bitterly painful for Diaghilev, seemed to him a symptom—not to say the expression—of the increasingly marked influence of American culture on the European scene.

That the "grand circle" of the international elites was being converted to cinema was a phenomenon that had not escaped Giuseppe Volpi's attention. Not long afterwards, he wouldn't hesitate to organize a Film Festival, staged on the terraces of the Excelsior Hotel facing the beach, to ideally link the Lido with Hollywood's entrepreneurial and intellectual universe.

———

Amidst this rapidly changing world, Palladio's *fabbrica*, which lies to the west of Venice, was seen—in its unchanging beauty and austere isolation—as a sort of alternative epicenter to the beaches and luxury hotels lying on Venice's eastern shores.

In this sense, a figure like Annina Morosini was probably seen—merely on account of her surname—as representing an aristocracy deeply rooted in the history of *La Serenissima*; moreover, her arrival reveals an interest in the historical dimension, which Bertie supposed might withstand the excitement of the beach seasons and the brilliant gimmicks (or publicity

Venice Film Festival, poster of the first edition of the Festival, 1932

Giuseppe Volpi and Piero Foscari, August 1904
Giuseppe Volpi, 1925
Marina Volpi, 1939

stunts) with which Elsa Maxwell tried to bring these two distant and separate worlds closer, and if possible to unite them.

This interest, together with a form of snobbism common to cosmopolitan circles, accounted for the fact that those Venetian patricians who could still be identified as such were invited to La Malcontenta. So were the illustrious members of Europe's leading noble families or figures of the caliber of Giuseppe Volpi (who was Mussolini's Finance Minister) or **Arthur Rubinstein**, all of whom were destined to leave their mark on history either in politics or for their extraordinary artistic abilities. (Moreover, the year before, Catherine had gone to Seville with Rubinstein to introduce her daughter Baba to the evocative charms of the *Feria*.)

Yet these acquaintances did not help Bertie to piece together information about the men who had commissioned Palladio to build this *palazzo*. The little that he managed to learn about the "magnificent brothers" Nicolò and Alvise Foscari scarcely satisfied his immense curiosity.[28] **Piero Foscari**, the nationalist leader who supported Giuseppe Volpi's early business ventures, the man behind the construction of the industrial port that was springing up just north of the city, and the senator of the kingdom and Under-Secretary of State, had died a year earlier.[29] His sons were too young to be involved in such sophisticated games.

Bertie did however manage to learn something about the last two family members who had lived in the *casa* in the years preceding the fall of the Venetian Republic. **Francesco Foscari**, an erudite scholar, had been Venice's ambassador first in Rome and later at the Sublime Porta, in Constantinople.[30] His son, **Ferigo**, was also kept at a distance by the other members of the Great Council of Venice who were worried about the political influence within the city of the descendants of the great Doge Francesco. For many years Ferigo was Ambassador at the court of Catherine the Great of Russia, in St Petersburg, and was then appointed to a no less challenging position as Ambassador to the Sultan.[31]

___

This dearth of historical information, which seemed objectively difficult to fill, had an extraordinary effect on Bertie who shifted his attention to a figure who was particularly distinctive on

J. Palma il Giovane, *Henri III arrives at Ca' Foscari*, detail
Domenico Farri, *Compositioni ... nella venuta in Venezia di Enrico III Re di Francia
e di Polonia*, Venice 1574

account of his character and noble standing, and who had chosen this *palazzo* for the first stop in a triumphal journey from Venice to Paris, where he was then crowned King of France.

In many ways **Henri III of Valois**, who had been King of Poland until 1574, evoked both Palladio and the name of the Foscari family.

He had been welcomed in Venice with solemn festivities that began at the coast, where a large Corinthian loggia had been erected to Palladio's design. Upon entering St Mark's basin, the king had passed under the central span of a triumphal arch "according to ancient custom," again designed by Palladio. He was then rowed up the Grand Canal on the *bucintoro*, the magnificent vessel reserved for the Doge's use, landing at the *casa granda* owned by the Foscari "on the bend of the Canal" (built by Francesco Foscari in the last years of his *dogado* [tenure as Doge]). On this occasion, the magnificently decorated house was occupied by Henri III, his *mignons* and a large court. However present during the day for reasons of protocol, the young French sovereign may have scarcely spent a single night there. While in Venice, the Frenchman sought out and enjoyed the homosexual pleasures that had been almost completely banned during the long months he had spent at the Polish court.

In Bertie's imagination, Henri III was an archetype for all subsequent visitors, with his conduct, his showy earring (which he continued to wear while in official mourning for his brother, the late king, from whom he had inherited the French crown), his flamboyant behavior and the disapproval that followed it, and the outrageous expenses incurred during his visit, all financed thanks to the loans offered by the Venetian Republic to ensure his supreme goodwill. Henri III became, for Bertie, a sort of royal emblem legitimizing exhibitionism and provocation, as well as spontaneity and license, an alternative model to any sort of conformism.

———

Another prime example of such eccentricity, and one that remained within the parameters of a bourgeois culture, was the **Marquess Luisa Casati** who came to symbolize a lifestyle that constantly verged on excess with surprising creativity.

Marquess Luisa Casati, 1922 (photo: Man Ray)

This unconventional woman, five years younger than Catherine, boasted somewhat androgynous looks which sufficed alone to turn heads wherever she went, even if she had not always been escorted by black servants and, as happened on more than one occasion, the odd panther, or had not showed up naked under billowing cloaks worn with no sense of inhibition. Her face was so heavily powdered that it seemed to be caked in lime, her eyes were thickly lined and her hair was dyed red. What piqued Bertie's, Catherine's and Paul's curiosity was the striking originality of a life that was deliberately lived as if it were a work of art. Luisa Casati had been pursued by **Gabriele D'Annunzio**, as Catherine had been courted by Morand; she had inspired works by **Filippo Tommaso Marinetti** and **Umberto Boccioni**; she had been painted by **Giovanni Boldini** and was soon to be immortalized by **Man Ray** in a notorious photograph that revealed the disturbing ambiguity of her sexual identity, and perhaps only became famous because of an error made while developing the negative. But these were not the only characteristics that interested Bertie, Catherine, and Paul.

Years earlier the Marquess had purchased a singular property, the unfinished Palazzo Venier "dei Leoni" (later to become Peggy Guggenheim's Venetian home). For all of fourteen years the Marquess used it as a sort of theatrical stage to display her flamboyant personality with a total lack of inhibition. Then, two years before Bertie's arrival in Venice, she sold the palace and moved to Paris, where she lived in the *Palais Rose*, which had belonged to the famous dandy Robert de Montesquiou (the *Baron de Charlus* immortalized by Marcel Proust). In short, Luisa Casati had shown how a house could be used in a manner that could be both unconventional and sophisticated. What was more, she had also thrown spectacular parties, to which she had invited nobility and nouveaux riches, the worlds of haute couture and provocation, culture and the theater, creating a highly effective, albeit ephemeral impact. For one of such parties she went as far as to rent St Mark's Square itself. These exploits and her other attributes had turned her into a living legend.

_____

Perhaps it was while talking to the Marquess Casati that Catherine decided to organize a grand social event, which she called *Notte a Venezia* (Night in Venice).

Catherine d'Erlanger, pamphlet for the ball at La Fenice on August 27, 1926, front cover

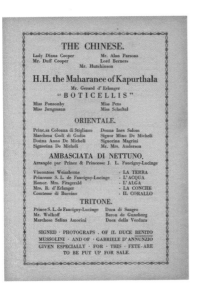

THE CHINESE.

Lady Diana Cooper   Mr. Alan Parsons
Mr. Duff Cooper   Lord Berners
    Mr. Hutchinson

H.H. the Maharanee of Kapurthala

Mr. Gerard d' Erlanger

"BOTICELLIS"

Miss Ponsonby   Miss Peto
Miss Jungmann   Miss Scheftel

ORIENTALE.

Princ.sa Colonna di Stigliano   Donna Ines Salom
Marchesa Godï di Godio   Signor Mino De Micheli
Donna Anna De Micheli   Signorina Magrini
Signorina De Micheli   Mr. Mrs. Anderson

AMBASCIATA DI NETTUNO.

Arrangée par Prince & Princesse J. L. Faucigny-Lucinge

Viscontess Weimborne   - LA TERRA
Princesse S. L. de Faucigny-Lucinge   - L'ACQUA
Honor. Mrs. Fitzgerald   - L'ALGA
Mrs. R. d'Erlanger   - LA CONCHE
Comtesse di Buccino   - IL CORALLO

TRITONE.

Prince S. L. de Faucigny-Lucinge   Duca di Sangro
Mr. Wolkoff   Baron de Gunzberg
Marchese Salina Amorini   Duca della Verdura

SIGNED · PHOTOGRAPS . OF IL DUCE BENITO
MUSSOLINI · AND OF · GABRIELE D'ANNUNZIO
GIVEN ESPECIALLY · FOR · THIS · FETE - ARE
TO BE PUT UP FOR SALE.

Théâtre "LA FENICE" - Venise

VENDREDI 27 AOUT 1926

La decorazione in vetro del palcoscenico - espres-
samente fatta per l'occasione - è creazione e opera
della M. V. M. CAPPELLIN & C. di Palazzo da
Mula - Murano.

Le Stoffe della Società Anonima FORTUNY

(GENTILMENTE OFFERTE)

STAMPERIA ZANETTI - VENEZIA

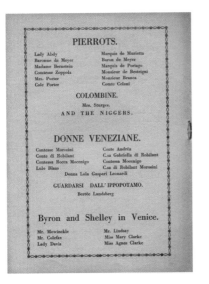

PIERROTS.

Lady Abdy   Marquis de Murietta
Baronne de Meyer   Baron de Meyer
Madame Bernstein   Marquis de Portago
Comtesse Zoppola   Monsieur de Besteigni
Mrs. Porter   Monsieur Branca
Cole Porter   Comte Celani

COLOMBINE.

Mrs. Sturges.

AND THE NIGGERS.

DONNE VENEZIANE.

Contesse Morosini   Conte Andréa
Conte di Robilant   C.sa Gabriella di Robilant
Contessa Rocca Mocenigo   Contessa Mocenigo
Lulo Blaas   C.sa di Robilant Morosini
    Donna Lola Gaspari Leonardi

GUARDARSI DALL' IPPOPOTAMO.

Bertàe Landsberg

Byron and Shelley in Venice.

Mr. Mowinckle   Mr. Lindsay
Mr. Colefax   Miss Mary Clarke
Lady Davis   Miss Agnes Clarke

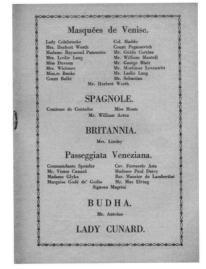

Masquées de Venise.

Lady Colebrooke   Col. Haddo
Mrs. Herbert Worth   Count Pogncsevich
Madame Raymond Patenotre   Mr. Guido Cortina
Mrs. Leslie Lang   Mr. William Mantell
Miss Duveen   Mr. George Blair
Mrs. Whitmer   Mr. Mortimer Leventritt
Miss.rn Banks   Mr. Leslie Lang
Count Balbi   Mr. Sebastian
    Mr. Herbert Worth

SPAGNOLE.

Comtesse de Contades   Miss Monts
Mr. William Acton

BRITANNIA.

Mrs. Lindsay

Passeggiata Veneziana.

Commandante Spender   Cav. Ferraccio Asta
Mr. Victor Cunard   Madame Paul Darcy
Madame Glyka   Bar. Maurice de Lambertini
Marquise Godé de' Godio   Mr. Max Elving
    Signora Magrini

BUDHA.

Mr. Antoine

LADY CUNARD.

Pages from the program for the ball at La Fenice

Her choice of La Fenice fo a venue, and desire that the celebrations re-enact the arrival of Byron and Shelley in Venice, highlight the differences between Catherine and the eccentric Marquess, or Linda and Cole, who hadn't hesitated to let the notes of the *Charleston* ring out over the Grand Canal.

To some extent Catherine's actions were tempered by a sort of awkwardness in relation to contemporary culture, as well as by the fact that her vanity was slightly dented by her own solid figure. Her individuality prevented her from such excessive exhibitionism in public, but her vitality offered the avant-garde an alternative way of life.

By inviting **Lady Colebrook**,[32] who was always in search of adventure, to help with the organization, Catherine hoped to overcome these qualms. Together they converted the *palazzina* of San Barnaba, which was already quite a dramatic setting, into their headquarters. Here they summoned a constant stream of friends and dressmakers. An external staircase led to the first floor, butting into the crenellated wall built expressly to lend the house a medieval appearance when seen from the outside. The first-floor hall, with its neo-Gothic decor, was transformed into changing rooms of an imaginary and provisional *atelier*. In the vast loggia on the ground floor a table was laid out with a lavish display of refreshments, while *chaises longues* were arranged to allow the guests to enjoy the coolness of the shady garden that was filled with oleanders, laurels, and a mimosa.

Those attending the ball at the Fenice were asked to wear fancy dresses or outfits that would evoke the period prior to 1850. In addition, to appease the more high-minded participants, a lottery was organized whose proceeds would be given to Venetian charitable institutions.

On the cover of the program announcing *Notte a Venezia*, Catherine included one of her own drawings, executed a little earlier, in 1922, as a sort of forerunner to *Art Déco*. She did so to remind those who were invited that she belonged to the circle of *Les Ballets Russes*, and to assert her independence from that artistic world which had affirmed its reputation at the *Exposition Internationale des Arts Décoratifs et Industriels Modernes*, which had been held in Paris the year before.

Another pamphlet, designed as a link to the Venetian figurative tradition, sported a rather unusual painting of a pachyderm by Pietro Longhi on the cover. This served to draw attention back to Bertie who had also put on a little weight in the past months and who was planning to attend the party dressed as a hippopotamus no less.

The invitation card specified: "At eleven o'clock, a herald will announce the entrance into the theater of the procession, made up of figures in magnificent fancy dress costumes, a dazzling array of styles from different countries and different historical periods." The procession was headed by a group of *Pierrots*, including Cole Porter and Linda.[33] **Cecil Beaton** was dressed as Harlequin. The all-black jazz band Linda hired—the ones who had shocked Diaghilev—followed "the Porters" dressed, somewhat incongruously, as Columbines. After them came the *Venetian Ladies*, including Annina Morosini who, on this occasion, was escorted by members of the Robilant family who were frequent guests at La Malcontenta.

Following the ladies, majestically and alone, came the *Hippopotamus*, whose real identity we now know.

There was no lack of costumed figures intended to conjure up Byron and Shelley's Venetian sojourn.[34] They were followed by the most varied groups, making up a procession of about a hundred people—whether titled figures, millionaires, or mere eccentrics—who composed that cosmopolitan universe formed by the remnants of the European aristocracy, and by the new social classes, which at the time were referred to in Paris as "le gratin révolté" (the eccentric upper crust of society).

The star of the party was obviously Catherine herself—who was now referred to by all as *Mimì*. She donated a gold chain to the lottery to encourage ticket sales. The fact that Prince of Faucigny-Lucinge was at her side, as was her daughter Baba, suffices to show that the event was intended to re-establish a link to the grand balls that had been held in Paris before the war. Above all, it was an ideal link to those genuine artistic happenings, hosted by Etienne de Beaumont in his private residence in Paris (the *hôtel particulier* built by the Prince de Masserano in the eighteenth century).

Cecil Beaton, self-portrait at the Lido dressed as Harlequin, 1926

Around the Palazzo

Catherine's plans for the ball were very tame compared to such sophisticated precedents: echoing a *retour à l'ordre* which in so many ways characterized the cultural moods of the tormented post-war years. This Venetian event lacked that blend of artists and aristocrats that sparked the Dada provocations only a few years earlier, the appearance of Malevic's "white square," and Raymond Roussel's "Chinese boxes." La Fenice Opera House, with its Austro-Hungarian décor, tempered any attempt to carry out unconventional experimentation. Yet, in spite of this, eccentricity and exhibitionism still managed to combine and merge in surprising ways at this event.

––––––

Throughout this whole period, Paul and Bertie remained aloof, somewhat in the background.[35] They were absorbed by the *palazzo* and by their desire to bring it back to life. Day after day, they embarked on long reconnaissance trips through the Veneto region, visiting "villas" and studying the layout of their gardens.

They realized that the successful reorganization of the land around Palladio's *palazzo* at Malcontenta would be a decisive step, and that it would enhance the excellence of the architecture.

Originally, perhaps as a concession to the gaining memento of the automobile at the time, they didn't rule out the possibility of building a road along the Riviera, not far from its banks, to allow guests to drive to the front of the house. However, they soon rejected this proposal as being too modernist, deciding instead to retain the navigable watercourse as the main access to the house, while the axial road built by Palladio to the south formed the secondary access.

This general layout then became the subject of lengthy reflection during which, as we imagine it, Bertie ideally took the part of the Sun King while Paul acted as Le Nôtre, the King's faithful gardener who devised avenues and parterres.

In this spirit, Paul then produced a long series of drawings through which the project for the garden gradually took shape. At a certain point, the axial road divided, after intersecting with a minor road, following a pattern that had been used in the past at Villa Emo in Fanzolo. There was a circle at the center of the intersection, in the middle of which Paul wanted to place a

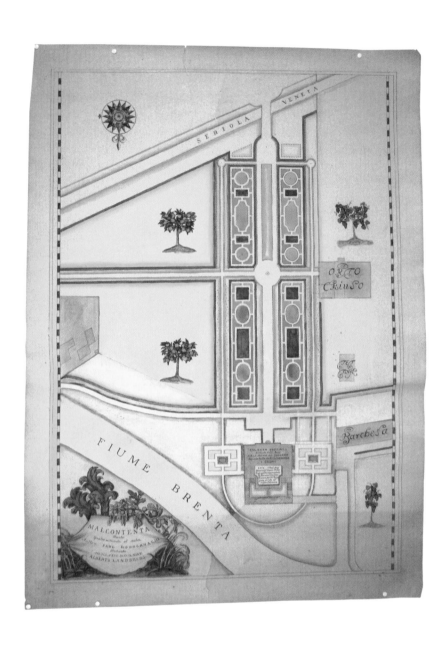

Paul Rodocanachi, general plan of the garden of La Malcontenta, 1926

Prince Jean-Louis of Faucigny-Lucinge in the garden of La Malcontenta
Paul Rodocanachi, design for a small labyrinth with a central pavilion at La Malcontenta
Catherine d'Erlanger, *Portrait of Paul Rodocanachi*

83

fountain, for which he promptly made a design, but this proved expensive and so in its intended place Bertie placed a small Venetian well. Parallel to this road system, and at some distance from it, were two pedestrian paths, which were grandly referred to as the *avenues*, flanked by an area of plants and shrubs that almost enclosed anyone walking along them, as if in a tunnel. These avenues stretched north and culminated in *giardini segreti* (private gardens) within which they formed a small labyrinth. Beyond these "gardens," the path circled in front of the *palazzo*.

This layout offered a sort of "guided tour" of the Palladian architecture. Visitors were, in a way, almost constrained to follow a shaded route that afforded rare glimpses of the *fabbrica*. They were then distracted, as they walked past the *palazzo*, by the small labyrinths, planted with sweet-scented plants. Moreover, the circular route offered a particular perception of the architecture, as if one was viewing it from a slow-moving boat floating round a bend in the Riviera in front of the *fabbrica*. It was almost obligatory to come to a halt on the axis of this extraordinary architecture, so compelling was the grandeur of the portico rising up in front of the façade, from which one could sense the complexity of the house's internal composition.

An inlet off the Riviera, and a small circular island, helped to ensure that the irregularly shaped grounds around the *palazzo* were formally balanced, even when viewed on a plan.

The large number of design iterations that Paul prepared for this scheme is an indication that this reflection on the layout of the grounds lasted not just for days but for weeks—perhaps even for an entire season. At the same time, the quality of the plans—the accuracy of the drawings, embellished with watercolors and cartouches bearing devoted dedications to the *Signore*—shows us how faithfully Paul played the role, which he'd taken upon himself, of *conseiller du roi* (king's advisor).

———

Paul showed the same thoughtfulness and sensitivity in guiding Bertie's first steps within the Palladian walls. But in this case, as we already know, Bertie already had a very clear notion of his own intentions.

He did not want to lose that sense, which he'd felt on first
entering the deserted building, that time had stood still, almost
as if he was holding his breath; he did not want to embark
upon any process of "historical invention," nor any display
of wealth which he did not own. He was jealous of the identity
of this house with which, by this stage, he felt entirely at
one. He wanted it to reflect his love. Not even electric light
would be allowed to dispel the penumbra which allowed such
feelings to transpire so poignantly in these rooms.

All the works, even the most important ones, were carried
out with the necessary caution, on the premise that they
should neither renew the old nor create a dialectic relationship
with it. Everything was to appear so natural that only a person
of refined culture would realize they were modern. Indeed,
if a visitor failed to notice them, their presence would only be
signaled by the questioning smile of the owner, watching the
person's face while accompanying him or her on a detailed tour
of the house.

The restoration had focused on the ground floor, already
compromised through inappropriate use, forgoing instead
the *piano nobile*, where nothing was to disturb the apprecia-
tion of the Palladian message.

Bertie chose (and here Paul's approval can be sensed
in the background) to emphasize the large central hall
as a place where the functions carried out in the side rooms
could converge; he also chose to underscore the specific
function of each room, using clever stratagems to interrupt any
remaining link between one room and the next.[36]

An old *tinello* (breakfast room), on the west side of the
casa, was transformed into a bathroom (an aspect which Paul
had resolved, in a particularly brilliant manner, in the house at
Neuilly). It was here that the large bath made from pink Verona
stone was installed: the one in which Cecil Beaton would
subsequently surprise Bertie photographing his naked body,
entirely covered with disconcerting tattoos.[37]

The central room, which was square in plan, retained
its historic function as a kitchen. However, steps were added
enabling one to look out of a window, which Palladio had
designed simply as a source of light. At the top of the steps
two niches were created where you could sit and wait for

La Malcontenta, ground floor, bathroom; central hall (photos: Osvaldo Boehm)

the sunset, enjoying the sight of the sun sliding down
behind the distant Euganean Hills. In the distance, maiolica
dishes and copper pots and pans on once limewashed
walls conjured up the appearance of the sixteenth-century
Venetian kitchens seen in old engravings.

The large room to the north, still on the west side of the
house, had rather an odd feel reminiscent of its past use
as a space for the most humble domestic tasks. In it were two
large plain wardrobes, which (according to Claud) came from
a cloister. A dozen or so people could eat together at a roughly
made table, supported on two trestles. A low wooden platform
under the table kept everyone's feet raised above the cold
damp floor.

Back in the large central cross-shaped hall, Bertie only allowed
pairs of objects: two sixteenth-century faldstools stood near
the ground-floor entrance (as if ready for use in the event that
the *Signore* might want to leave the house escorted by his
sediari [chair-carriers]). Little further away, two wooden sculp-
tures (from an eighteenth century Venetian theater), that were
promptly christened Rinaldo and Armida stood by a drop of
the floor level.[38]

Bertie's use of the two fine antique octagonal tables is a
good example of his rigor in applying Palladio's rule of symmetry to the building. First installed in the two arms of the cross,
where they did not look right, the tables were sawn in half to
make four wall tables, which were then used to furnish all four
arms of the cross-shaped hall.

At the center of the axis running along the architectural
composition hung a large lamp, which could be lowered when
necessary to change the wick by untying the large rope on
which it was suspended.

Only vague rumors of these operations reached Venice.
However, they were enough to whet the curiosity of Cole Porter
who arrived on October 2, immediately after the ball held at
La Fenice. On this occasion he was not with Gerald and Sara
Murphy, who in the meantime had moved to the Côte d'Azur
where they set the fashion of wearing striped fishermen's
vests and *espadrillas*, inviting Picasso and Fitzgerald to follow
them. Instead Porter was accompanied by **Carlo Ruspoli**,

the Roman prince who had married Giuseppe Volpi's eldest daughter **Marina Volpi**.

Giuseppe Volpi himself also visited in October, accompanied by **Ettore Tito** (the painter who was then decorating the ballroom ceiling in Volpi's Venetian palace). The talented businessman, who was then at the height of his ministerial mandate, was baffled by the simplicity with which these three people—an Anglicized Brazilian, a Frenchified Greek, and a French noblewoman full of Mediterranean exuberance—lived in a building which still appeared to be in a state of neglect. While referring to them as "saviors," he could not restrain himself from encouraging them to undertake a more substantial restoration. "What is done," he wrote before adding his assertive signature to the visitors' book, "guarantees what will be done to honor *our* Palladio with devotion."

The sense of bewilderment Volpi felt during his visit is in some ways enlightening. It reveals how difficult it was, at that time, for Italians to understand the concept of preservation that was maturing in Bertie's mind in response to the intrinsic beauty of the Renaissance masterpiece to which he had decided to dedicate his life. It is as if the interventions carried out by Bertie and Paul were of such lightness and formal appropriateness that they were scarcely perceptible, even to a man like Volpi, who lacked neither intelligence nor acuity.

———

In Bertie's understanding of conservation, everything was seen as a historical document: not only the structures of the villa, but also, in so far as was possible, its atmosphere, which was the product of over a century's neglect. The building—of this he was convinced—must not be modernized; it must not be subjugated to functionality, privacy, and comfort, namely to cultural requirements that no one was even aware of at the time it was built. Any form of modernization would have compromised its historical identity and altered our perception of the prophecy of modernity, evinced, and perhaps even breathed, in these rigorously designed spaces. Even electric light—as we know now—was deemed incompatible with the architecture's quintessential.

Let us draw a fuller picture of exactly what Giuseppe Volpi saw on the *piano nobile* of this *palazzo*.

The only furniture in the rooms were "straw" chairs and boxes on which to sit, described Paul Morand (who in the meantime had married **Princess Soutzo**, on the basis that she never objected to his endless sentimental peccadilloes and as she owned a considerable number of oil wells in Romania). Indeed, Morand came to La Malcontenta almost immediately hoping to pursue Catherine for the emotional pleasures that she alone, clearly, could bring to those who valued her extraordinary vitality.

"At the centre of the Latin cross," Morand later wrote, remembering his visit in the summer of 1927, "a ping-pong table was laid out with all the fruits from Rialto, on maiolica plates purchased in the local flea market."[39]

The meeting on July 20th, 1928, at which Morand was also present, "was in part Plato's Banquet and in part the Abbey of Thelema."[40] **José Maria Sert**, who was already familiar with these rooms (as he also visited after the great party at La Fenice), had collapsed into a sagging armchair, with his two wives, Misia and Roussy, stretched out at his feet.[41]

Diaghilev—whose single lock of white hair stood out from an otherwise visibly dyed hair—was recumbent on a divan, lying absolutely still on his back for a long time, peering through his monocle at the whitewash covering the walls. He was trying to discover where the painting cycle depicting Philemon and Baucis could be, the performance of *Philémon et Baucis* he had directed two years earlier in Monte Carlo clearly still in his mind. On that occasion the loyal Alexandre Benois had come to the rescue at short notice when Picasso announced that he could not provide the scenery for the performance in time.

In the meantime Catherine, "who had the knack of mobilizing all her lovers—past, present, and future—and making them live together," prompted Kochno and Lifar to expose the figures, which were still hidden under a layer of whitewash. While they were at work, Catherine helped them and, whenever a new fragment of the antique decoration was revealed, she shouted in excitement: "It's a Paolo! It's a Paolo!" By this she meant of course Paolo Veronese, a name that intensified the excited atmosphere that greeted each new discovery.

Catherine d'Erlanger and Oliver Messel in the central hall (photo: Cecil Beaton)

Catherine d'Erlanger and Oliver Messel in the portico (photo: Cecil Beaton, detail)

Re-evoking this scene, a year later, Cecil Beaton photographed **Oliver Messel** standing in his ballet shoes on top of a ladder, intent on scraping off the whitewash covering the frescos. Catherine d'Erlanger was again at the foot of the ladder, ready to hand him—as she had done for Kochno and Serge Lifar—a goblet of champagne and some exquisite paté spread on slices of bread bought from the baker in La Malcontenta.

The days went by quickly in this climate of excitement. There was no let up, even when news reached the Riviera that Cole Porter was forced to leave Venice. The Mayor had decreed him as *persona non grata* after a police raid on the Palazzo Rezzonico had discovered a "river" of cocaine and Cole, in the company of a dozen or more young Venetians, dressed—when they were—in Linda's own gowns, while she was away in Paris.

————

Winston Churchill arrived on the scene in October. He was just over fifty at the time and was Chancellor of the Exchequer in Stanley Baldwin's Conservative government. He was accompanied by **Clementine**, his wife, who had already been in Venice for several weeks, convalescing from an accident she had suffered in June. **Fredrick Alexander Lindemann**, a chemistry professor, was also with him. The latter was supposed to help Churchill understand the production strategy that had led to the construction of major chemical plants in the areas just north of La Malcontenta, in the industrial area around Porto Marghera, which was almost completely under Volpi's control.

In order to please this Minister of the British government (which was reasonably well disposed towards Mussolini at the time), Giuseppe Volpi promptly ordered the construction of a golf course on the large areas of land owned by the state on the southern tip of the Lido. Nothing was left to chance: he appointed Cruickshank, a Scottish golf course designer with an established track record, and asked him to create a particularly stunning course, at record speed.[42]

By this stage our *ménage à trois*—recognized as such by the many European celebrities whose company they kept—had little concerns about presenting themselves as a threesome in society. This is what occurred at the ball given by **Count Andrea di Robilant** in his three adjoining palaces

Paul Morand (left) dressed as Baron de Charlus and others;
Elsa Maxwell and the Countess of Robilant, Proust Ball, Paris 1928

overlooking the Grand Canal. Amidst the flurry of guests
who had been summoned to Venice, Bertie appeared, in grand
style, dressed as a Roman warrior. Elsa Maxwell came as
Diaghilev and, as an ironic comment on Diaghilev's known
aversion for American culture, she was escorted by a *troupe*
of black dancers.[43]

This gathering of "high society" then migrated to Paris
where they were all invited to the ball—intended as an homage
to Marcel Proust—which Baba, together with Prince of
Faucigny-Lucinge, gave in her *hôtel particulier.*[44]

Perhaps all these parties—which were to some extent,
extraneous to the bond that united Paul, Catherine and Bertie—
started to dispel the enchantment, foregoing their indissoluble
link. Or perhaps it was something else.

Yet something had upset their delicate balance. This is evident
from a clue that appears in the visitors' book at the end of
September 1928. In his clear hand, Paul wrote three words
(in Italian) that alone reveal the tension in his mind. Addressing
Bertie, he wrote, "con rispetti servili" (with obsequious
regards). Bertie then nervously scrawled "Dear idiot" in sharp
retort to Paul's short but stinging comment. Presumably his
intention was to call his friend to order with an expression that
revealed his disapproval, but nonetheless underscores the
bond that united them.

To grasp Paul's underlying crisis, it is important to
consider how his move to the banks of the Brenta, however
seasonal it was, had to some extent undermined his ability to
identify with the house in Rue du Centre, which had symbolized
the epicenter of his psychological equilibrium and his way
of life for over thirty years.

A symptom of this encroaching crisis of this kind had
occurred in August 1926 when Paul had agreed for photographs
of his house—namely of the intimate and segregated world
of his private life—to be published in a popular magazine illustrating a long and descriptive article.[45]

If, on the one hand, this had prompted Paul to regard
his life in Neuilly-sur-Seine as coming to an end, on the other
it was clear that his unique gift for inventing forms to revive
and exalt the splendor of the past had not yet found an outlet

Hôtel Rodocanachi, dining-room; bathroom, 1926

for expression at La Malcontenta; nor would they ever have been without overriding the particular theory of conservation that had developed and then established itself in Bertie's mind, to the point of becoming a fully fledged philosophy.

Having come to the end of the first exciting—and one might say heroic—phase, in which Paul had found fulfillment acting as advisor to his young Sun King, his responsibilities were now limited to the *mise en place* of the few rare objects which Bertie allowed to be brought within the Palladian walls on account of their aesthetic qualities or evocative powers. Otherwise, Paul's role was limited, almost exclusively, to preparing decorations destined to last for a single evening.

For example, when Paul completed a drawing in preparation for the display of some or other ornament—a small tray, a sixteenth century box for holding old bottles, firedogs to be fitted with brass knobs taken from the railings of some old staircase, a footrest to be placed in front of an armchair—Bertie no longer refrained from penning his comments or adding hastily (and sometimes badly) written dimensions, as if perfectly proportioned and measured drawings were not sufficiently clear instruction for the craftsman entrusted to create it. This state of affairs was a crisis waiting to happen.

On September 19, 1927 Boris Kochno reappeared at La Malcontenta accompanied, in addition to **Balanchine**, by a young man who literally burst into Paul's life. **Arturo-José Lopez-Willshaw** was a twenty-seven year old Chilean, with large light-colored eyes that almost seemed made-up. He looked like Bertie might have ten years earlier, except for the rather childish gaze on his face.

Paul could not resist the temptation to adopt this young South American as his pupil, just as he done with Bertie. He invited him to his house in Neuilly-sur-Seine, which to some extent he regarded as his intimate portrait and which continued to be the setting in which he found himself most at ease, and where he felt most confident in his actions.

Inevitably, Arturo-José was also captivated by the charm of the house in Rue du Centre and its owner. Paul resolved to create a binding tie with this young man. Not long afterwards he signed a contract in which he leased him the house for

six years including the right of first refusal should he decide
to sell it. Paul became Arturo-José's mentor, in the same way
that he had been to Bertie. To do so, he undertook to reinvest
the entire rent on improvements to the house (while reserving
the right to walk in "his" garden, and also the right to use
an apartment in the house, namely the service flat, which he had
created only a short time earlier, above the garage).[46]

Paul's passion for the young Chilean and the latter's
sudden transformation were manifestly obvious to anyone who
spent time with them. For this reason, Arturo-José's father—
a man who owned the guano quarries supplying the finest
fertilizer in his country—had no other choice, given the cosmopolitan high society of which he too was part, but to buy the
house and gift it to his son. This duly happened, on the pretext
of Arturo-José's imminent twenty-eighth birthday.

Yet, instead of being completed by June, the sale
was held up and still had not gone through by late August.
This explains why Paul was agitated in early September.
His ego was profoundly disturbed. Staying at La Malcontenta
in some way constrained him limiting his freedom, if only
psychologically. Bertie tried to keep him there by inviting
Roger Quilter, in the hope of re-establishing that equilibrium,
which for many years had characterized their relationship.
But even the arrival of his long-cherished friend could not calm
the worries that weighed on Paul's mind.

The sale was not finalized until November 5, 1928.[47]
A portrait of a happy, almost triumphant Arturo-José was
commissioned to celebrate this event, holding open in front of
him a large sheet of paper depicting his new house. In a corner
of this sheet was an ornate scroll of leaves, embellished
by an occasional red berry. It read: "House of Mr Arturo Lopez/
Architect Paul Rodocanachi/1928."

The year 1928 was anxious in all respects. Agitation was
in the air, and no one knew what it might produce, or where
it might lead. As a result of the tremors shaking the world at
large, the visitors flocked to the villa on the banks of the Brenta
with even greater regularity than before.

Paul Rodocanachi, sketches of various objects; design of a glass bowl

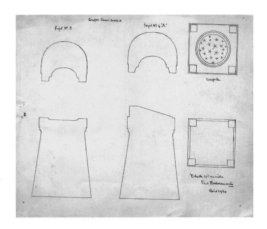

Serge Lifar in a gondola at Serge Diaghilev's funeral, Venice 1929 (t.l.)
Paul Rodocanachi, design for Serge Diaghilev's tomb, 1930 (t.r.)
Arturo-José Lopez-Willshaw, 1927 (b.l.)
Alexander Evgenievich Yakovlev, *Arturo-José Lopez-Willshaw* (b.r.)

Roger Quilter, Bertie Landsberg, Catherine d'Erlanger,
and Ettore Stefani at La Malcontenta, 1928

Terrace at Carlos de Beistegui's house, Paris 1930 (photos: Le Corbusier)

A Mexican gentleman arrived at least twice. He, too, was
extremely rich and, in his own way, he was an emblem of
how society, or at least some of its most prominent members,
lived through this turning point between a past that was at
hand and a future that had not yet taken shape. Aged just over
thirty, **Carlos de Beistegui** was a "man of the world." He
had not missed Catherine's ball at La Fenice (taking part in the
fancy dress parade, dressed as a Pierrot, alongside Cole and
Linda Porter).

Rather than rushing off to social events during these
turbulent months, this multi-millionaire—as it was said at the
time—sought out **Le Corbusier** asking him to test his *toit-jardin*
(roof garden) theories on the roof of his Parisian home. At the
time Le Corbusier was building that superb masterpiece which
is Villa Savoye, in Poissy; he grasped the paradox expressed by
Carlos de Beistegui and proceeded to create an experimental
construction imbued with extraordinary surrealist suggestions.

––––––––

Diaghilev's death, in hindsight, was also a turning point.
On an oppressively hot August day in 1929, Diaghilev passed
away in Hôtel des Bains (he was naturally spending the
summer, once again, at the Lido di Venezia) having been unable
to resist the five-course meals that his doctors had severely
warned him against on account of the dangerously advanced
stage of his diabetes. He died in the arms of Serge Lifar, and
in the presence of Kochno and Misia Sert. Having heard
of Diaghilev's worsening conditions, she had hastened to reach
Venice on board the Duke of Westminster's yacht, the *Flying
Cloud*, on which she and Coco Chanel had been invited to
a cruise down the Dalmatian coast, on the far side of the Gulf
of Venice.

With characteristic dynamism, which she possessed
even at the saddest moments, Catherine overcame her grief
by throwing herself into making the arrangements for Diaghilev's
funeral. Having collected money from his friends (even
from Misia), she organized a water-borne procession that
departed from the Greek church, where a sad and crowded
funeral was held, gliding slowly across the lagoon to the island
Napoleon had designated to be Venice's cemetery. As a
Russian, Diaghilev was buried in the sector reserved for those

of Orthodox faith. Catherine secured a plot on the eastern
edge of the graveyard, from which, over the wall separating the
cemetery from the lagoon, one could watch the sun rise behind
the coastline. There was slight consternation during the
burial of the coffin, as Serge Lifar attempted to follow the fate
of his master by throwing himself into the grave, and was only
restrained by Kochno with difficulty.

Paul, who had been brought up, as a child, in the Orthodox
faith, designed a square pillar on which stood a sort of miniature
ciborium, topped by a small cupola on a square base for
the tomb of the *Ballet Russe's* founder. Catherine made the
arrangements for its construction providing the necessary funds.

———

Meanwhile, work on the road bridge, which had been initiated
by Giuseppe Volpi to flank the rail bridge between Mestre
and Venice, progressed at pace. Shortly it, too, would link the
city even more firmly to the *terraferma*, definitively violating
the insular nature of *La Serenissima*.

Animated once again by what seemed like irrepressible
fervor, Catherine was enthusiastic enough to visit the building
works, which she likened to a Faustian scene; in her excitement
at seeing the site, she was convinced that the opening of
the bridge—to be called the Ponte del Littorio in celebration of
the Fascist regime—would persuade many of the tourists,
who would now be drawn to Venice, to visit La Malcontenta
where they could admire the Palladian masterpiece reflected
in the waters of the Brenta. In anticipation of this she set the
admission price to the mysterious *palazzo*, of which many had
now heard, at three lire.

The leaflet, which was printed to mark the opening
of the new road bridge at a ceremony attended by the Principi
di Piedmont, highlighted the possibility of visiting the Renaissance *fabbrica* while also mentioning the excellence of the
meat and eggs that were on sale beside the majestic building
erected by Palladio four centuries earlier. The truth of the
matter was that Catherine was finding it difficult to sell the
produce from the chickens that she herself had suggested
breeding, and for which she had ordered the construction
of a real henhouse in front of the *barchessa* (outbuilding used
as barn or farm building) at the villa.

The Great Depression

Indeed, not long before, Catherine, whose curiosity was boundless, had attended an international agricultural exhibition in Rome where she had been fascinated by the feathers of the most eye-catching cockerels and by the variety of species on show. In her enthusiasm, she wasted no time in buying the prize-winning cockerels with the most astonishing plumage, as well as a large number of hens of the same kind.

There is no doubt that even Cecil Beaton, the Marquess Casati and Misia Sert, as well as the other visitors to Venice who decided to make the journey to La Malcontenta that summer, would have had Catherine dutifully escort them to visit her henhouse. However, it was Bertie who, in his own way, advertised the enterprise by displaying colored reproductions of pictures of all kinds of cockerels, with their haughty and proud looks, inside the doors of the two large cupboards, which stood wide open when he dined with guests in the large room on the ground floor. Even Elizabeth T.F. Courtauld and Grace Lovat Fraser, who visited the villa purely out of cultural interest, would have found it impossible not to notice this sort of advertising.

———

However, the crisis that would bring down the financial markets—after so much excitement, eccentricity, and frivolity—was now imminent.

In late October the panic on Wall Street spread throughout the world. Catherine promptly withdrew to her house in Piccadilly. Paul returned to Paris throwing himself body and soul into the refurbishment of the house in Rue du Centre: he wanted to prove to Arturo-José that he still had the gift of reinventing the past and manipulating forms. He set to with enthusiasm, almost with determination, as if an operation of this kind alone could exorcize the upheaval that was now affecting European culture, and could reverse the onset of that modernity that would displace (he understood this better than many others) the very cultural references that inspired his management of space and the decoration of a house.

Contrary to any sense of rationalism, functionalism, or pragmatism, Paul planned each room in the house, which he was now reinterpreting for this new phase of his life—the music room, the dining room, the bedroom, the room reserved for performances by the male dancers—as if each were the setting for a discipline that had to be exercised with the utmost rigor, and taken to an extreme. In such a particular conception, pleasures were to be cultivated with a ritual that was no less strict than that reserved for the exercise of duty.

In this new incarnation, the house in Rue du Centre started to become "a miniature Versailles" (to use Cecil Beaton's words). Paul once more took on the role of advisor to the king, which he found congenial, and like Le Nôtre with Louis XIV, he allowed his reigning sovereign to choose from his most precious and most beautiful objects.

Yet these objects would cease to have any utility when used to decorate the rooms of this virtual royal palace: here there could only be works of art. Whether they were made by goldsmiths, cabinetmakers, or other fine craftsmen, what mattered was that the works had to form an ensemble, which could then grow into a collection.[48]

Stimulated by such specific and intense guidance, the education of Paul's pupil soon reached a level that would otherwise have been unattainable, at least in such a short time. Cecil Beaton would later write, in a work that was published many years later: "Since Mr Lopez-Willshaw is, I believe, a South American of great wealth, he has been able to devote much of his time to the search for unique pieces, and his knowledge has become infallible. If his taste treads little new ground in its grandeur of style and perfection of theatrical effect, it at least continues to keep open the path trodden by Largillière.... To look at the house in Neuilly, one can hardly believe this transformation scene is of recent development."[49]

The end of 1929 was also marked by the onset of an extremely harsh winter in Venice. It was as if the city, so different to all others, reacted in its own way to the crisis that gripped the world's financial markets by turning the bitter cold into crystal. However, to Bertie, the cold weather offered a panoply of new aesthetic experiences. He was fascinated by the sight of the frozen lagoon, which he photographed on numerous occasions, and he was inspired to hunt for old engravings and reproductions of seventeenth- and eighteenth-century paintings depicting equally spectacular *gelate* (frozen scenes). Until then, he had only seen the lagoon in its normal conditions.

Indeed, he had explored its ever-changing amphibious nature in a *sandolo* (a traditional flat-bottomed Venetian rowing boat), together with **Luigi Conton**, searching for evidence of the materials—mainly broken and discarded pottery—used by the Venetians during the fifteenth and sixteenth centuries to build new embankments or to reinforce the oldest ones.[50]

At this point—as if to make up for the absence of Paul's warm voice—Bertie befriended, not without some hesitation, those whom he had never felt the need to contact earlier. He welcomed, among others, **Antonio Maraini**, the versatile intellectual whom Giuseppe Volpi had invited to manage the Biennale when he became chairman. Maraini arrived on the banks of the Riviera in the summer of 1931, just after closing an exhibition at which the Italians were able to discover Modigliani and Henry Moore; he was preparing another at which, alongside an exhibition of Italian artists in Paris (featuring De Chirico, De Pisis, Campigli and Severini), he would present a review of Futurist aerial painters (Prampolini and Depero, as well as Severini). Bertie realized that this "director", whom he may have criticized for his overly obsequious politeness to members of the Italian government, played a highly proactive cultural role on the Venetian scene.

However, Bertie's decision to stay in touch with the Italian artistic scene did not suffice to banish the feeling of loneliness that preoccupied and also tormented him during these months. Paul was well aware of this and he gave Bertie part of the proceeds from the sale of the house in Neuilly (it had sold for 2,750,000 French francs) since he was uncomfortably aware of the difference between Arturo-José's and "poor Bertie's financial circumstances."

———

Certainly Paul and Bertie would have talked about removing the layer of whitewash to reveal what was left of the grandiose decorative cycle, which covered the walls and ceilings of all the rooms on the *piano nobile* of this palace. Likewise they would also have questioned whether or not the operation could enhance the "quality" of the Palladian building.

They frequently asserted that the whiteness of the plaster enhanced the rigor of the architecture in these rooms, and rendered the harmony governing the dimensions of each space

Bertie Landsberg at La Malcontenta in the winter of 1929

La Malcontenta, central hall (photo: Osvaldo Boehm)

more clearly perceptible. In the large central hall some figures were just visible, and their fragmentary state was highly evocative. The layer of whitewash covering the walls could also be likened to a veil, which concealed a mystery, and this added to the fascination of a building that was already imbued with enigmatic messages. The attempts made by his guests, who were urged on by Catherine, to reveal these frescos was motivated by nothing more than a sinful—and therefore exciting—temptation to violate this mystery. The descriptions of the decorative cycle left by earlier art historians—by Ridolfi and by Boschini—merely fired their imagination, perhaps even more than any tangible evidence of the figures would have done.

The layer of whitewash obscuring the frescos was later removed, and with it any possible objection. This operation was conceived to counterbalance that fervor of modernization taking place on the banks of the Seine, at the house in Neuilly.

Yet Bertie did not allow himself to be carried away by the excitement; he intended to be guided by prudence. He knew that architecture and painting are two separate media, often at loggerheads with one another. Above all, he knew that revealing the ancient decorative cycle, which covered the walls and ceilings of all the rooms, would be like introducing music into spaces whose only embellishment had been, and still was, one of prolonged silence.

He had to avoid repeating the mistake made in 1908 by Hierschel de Minerbi who, to save money, had brought in completely untrained workmen to "restore" the *stanza grande* in the western wing, with extremely disappointing results. The gaps left by the removal of many frescos during the intervening years were a distressing sight. Above all, the deterioration now included the image of that sumptuously dressed female figure who was seen, by those of a romantic inclination, as the *malcontenta* (unhappy woman) held captive in penitence for her passionate love affairs, in penitence with her social status as a married woman.

To avoid such unfortunate results Bertie called in a "professor" who could oversee the restoration of the decorative cycle in the *stanza grande* on the east side. But, as is often the case when one changes course in order to solve a problem, one runs into a problem of the opposite kind. **Arturo Raffaldini**

La Malcontenta, room of Aurora (t.l.); room of Prometheus (r.);
room of *The Fall of the Giants* (b.r., photos: Osvaldo Boehm)

The Fall of the Giants at La Malcontenta (photo: Osvaldo Boehm)

restored the frescos so carefully as to erase those traces of time, which instead serve as an eloquent testimony of the history of this house and the damage it incurred during the many years of abandonment. Above all, when the work was finished the restoration of the architectural details proved to be fastidiously reconstructive.

The decision to place a four-poster bed in this room was in many ways a consequence of Bertie's discomposure, since the reconstructive nature of the operation ran contrary to his deepest convictions about the very essence of restoration.

Finding a large bed in this *stanza grande* proved bewildering for anyone—namely most of the guests visiting the house—not familiar with how these old houses were used, but it distracted attention from the overly radical restoration of the frescos. Moreover, the bedhead covered quite a large lacuna in the decorative cycle on the wall opposite the large fireplace in red Verona stone, which Palladio had carefully built to bring warmth and comfort to all who slept in front of it here in this room.

Paul designed this bed, but Bertie guided his work, knowing precisely what he didn't want. He did not want a re-evocation of the Baroque rituals, which Paul had introduced into the house in Rue du Centre, where Arturo-José's bed stood on a raised dais inside an alcove protected by a balustrade, like the focal point on a real stage-set. Nor did he want an antique bed: with its alien history, a period bedstead might have broken the suspension of time (of all eras), which one breathes in a house straddling the past and future. Nor did he want a copy of a classical bed.

Here, in front of the great fireplace, Bertie envisioned a Renaissance bed. Furthermore, he wanted this metaphor to take shape without going against those rules of economy—or rather, parsimony—that had governed all the operations undertaken up to this point.

Paul had no difficulty in interpreting the *Signore*'s expectations. He designed the *cassone* (a sort of platform) that would support the bed and serve as a place to store blankets, sheets, and other linen, as was the custom in the past. This platform composed of wooden planks was put together so simply that the village carpenter was charged with its realization. Therefore the elegance of this item of furniture was entirely, and solely, conceptual. The only decorative element was the thin, fluted columns standing at the corners of the *cassone*. These were topped by gilded wooden balls (again made from simple pinewood).

Bertie and Paul did not hesitate to fit the room with a commode, placed beside the large window through which the morning light streamed in. In particular, they took mischievous pleasure in disguising it as an unusual armchair, which stood on a wooden platform.[51]

———

The reason why Bertie did not then shun the "professor" who had carried out a restoration that Bertie found unsatisfactory was that Raffaldini, who was from Mantua, had worked in the Palazzo Te, the residence built by **Giulio Romano** for the ruling Gonzaga family, just outside the city walls. It was here, in a large square room, that Romano had painted the famous *Fall of the Giants*, a spectacular depiction of the ruinous end of the sons of the goddess Earth after they had dared to scale Mount Olympus, thereby arousing Jupiter's fury.

This same theme was the subject of the frescos in the square room on the east side of La Malcontenta. The room's walls featured the bodies of the *Zigantoni* (as Boschini called the giants),[52] "all pride, vigor, and alertness," yet still "in limbo" (to quote Bernard Berenson's felicitous phrase) because they were hidden by a veil of whitewash.[53]

As the restorer gradually uncovered the body of a first *Colossus*, who "in anger and fury leapt onto them,"[54] Bertie's enthusiasm knew no bounds and he was prompted to position a large white ceramic obelisk in front of the figure. This was in fact a nineteenth-century Austrian stove whose hot air would be used to heat the room, flowing through the chimney flue.[55]

However, beyond this momentary excitement, Bertie's intellectual curiosity in this iconography drawn from Ovid's *Metamorphoses* proved long-lasting. Much later, in the context of illustrating the decorative cycle adorning the walls of the *piano nobile*—by **Giambattista Zelotti** and **Batista Franco**—his writing is as insightful as that of any art critic.[56]

The Wooden Scaffolding

Joyous from the re-discovery of the *Fall of the Giants*, Bertie
thought he could embark on the restoration of the decorative
cycle embellishing the walls and ceiling of the large cruciform
room in the center of the house.

To do so, the large room had to be completely emptied.
Everything had to go, even the fruit boxes, which Paul Morand
had seen being used as chairs, and the ping-pong table with
its trays of seasonal fruit.

As the furnishings were gradually removed, the space
assumed an even greater dignity: it reacquired that sense
of emptiness which is the essence of an architecture free from
objects, of a civilization that precedes those forms of con-
sumerism which, as the centuries passed, would generate a
be-wildering accumulation of furniture and ornaments.

Pursuing a dream, which he could share with only
a few others, Bertie found this immensely gratifying. What
was more, he sensed that these Renaissance spaces were
incompatible with all forms of furnishing, especially after
he could finally ascertain that the fresco decoration, which
was just visible in the vaulted ceiling of the cruciform room,
extended all the way to the floor. This confirmed that Palladio
must have intended that the walls should be free of furniture.

Instead of looking out of place, or even unsuited to this complex
and solemn space, the wooden scaffolding, which was erected
to allow the restorers to do their work, proved to be very
congenial—perhaps because, in some way, it conjured up the
appearance of Palladio's building site when the vaults were
being built, or perhaps because it was here, on scaffolding like
this, that Palladio's assistants would have worked, clambering
over these rudimentary structures in order to carry plaster,
paints, and even wine and loaves to their "masters." However,
the latter had to be consumed rapidly in order not to interrupt
the work that had to be finished during the short time that
the plaster remained *fresco* (wet): each *giornata* or day's work
had to be completed by sunset.[57]

Aside from any other suggestion, the fact that the
scaffolding looked appropriate in such a large space can also
be attrib-uted to the fact that it constituted a sort of theatrical
machine. It enabled Bertie to treat the operation as a perfor-

mance, one that generated the excitement of new discoveries each day and therefore prompted comments and raised questions (about the artist who had done the work, the iconographical meaning of each figure, the procedures to be used in their restoration, and the level of finish to be attained).

It hardly matters that, in the end, the restoration was never carried out because Bertie realized that he lacked the means.

Moreover, the members of what remained of the Venetian patriciate and those aristocrats who could contribute knowledge and information—for no other reason than that some still owned villas on the Venetian mainland—were regularly summoned to witness this ephemeral spectacle. A succession of members of the Valmarana, Dolfin Boldù, Moro-Lin, Mocenigo, Emo Capodilista, Roi, Piovene, Nani Mocenigo, and de Lazara Pisani families, amongst others, walked into the room and stared up at the ceiling. We also know that one of Piero Foscari's sons was present: Adriano was a naval officer with a brilliant career, and during the Second World War he would be honored with a gold medal for bravery in action on the Mediterranean.

This informal procession didn't interrupt the almost regular sequence of royal visits, made by members from those rather precarious dynasties still in power to the east of the Adriatic (the royal houses of Greece, Romania, Serbia and Montenegro), as well as Catherine's relatives and long-established friends. One such was **Princess Bibesco**, for example, who wrote in the visitors' book as a testimonial of her visit the words conceived by Heinrich Heine, in the hope that they might be engraved on her tomb if it were ever placed in the villa's garden: "Il aime les roses de la Brenta."

As for his own guests—above all, those arriving for the first time—Bertie welcomed them in the center of the pronaos. He did so also to ensure that each visitor was obliged to follow the principles of Palladio's design: namely, that they should admire the surprising appearance of the outline of a "temple" on the house's façade, that they should hesitate for a moment before choosing which stairs to take in order to ascend to the *piano nobile*, and lastly, once inside the imposing portico, that they should rediscover the axis of symmetry which governed the composition of the *fabbrica*.

He left each new arrival time to recover from the shock of discovering the totally unexpected yet imposing space beyond the great entrance, closed by a door made of simple wooden planks, worn by time. He then offered each a glass of vermouth, almost always without a word.

The vermouth, a white Martini, contained a curl of lemon rind added by the faithful housekeeper taken from the lemons, as Bertie always hastened to add, that grew in the large terracotta pots, which he re-introduced to embellish the garden overlooked by the south-facing façade, reinstating a custom first introduced by Venetian patricians at their villas during the seventeenth century. Like the two luxuriant jasmines growing on either side of the ground-floor door, this was also a way of using southern scented plants to enrich an architecture that, in the eyes of many Anglo-Saxon visitors, seemed in many respects more Mediterranean than Latin.

When Bertie encountered a guest who seemed to be better informed or more engaging than others, he would expound his theories of Italian Renaissance architecture and tell them, with renewed enthusiasm, how this building gave him a sense of adventure. He was so adept at expressing his enthusiasm that **Osbert Sitwell**, a writer of extraordinary talent, promptly dedicated a chapter in his travel diary to the results of Bertie's research on Palladio's architecture.[58]

After walking through the rooms on the *piano nobile*, Bertie then accompanied his guest to the ground floor, and never failed to address the subject of "conveniences," a topic that he took delight in mentioning since it was generally skirted around in well-to-do conversation. He mentioned that Palladio had stated that lavoratories should be built off the stairs, because this ensured enough draught to avoid any lingering malodors.

During the winter months, when even the restorers could not continue their work because their hands were stiff with cold, that Bertie, Catherine and Paul would return to Paris. There they explored the length and breadth of the city, following a guide written by Catherine's brother a few years earlier.[59] Some weeks later, Bertie and Catherine would move to London.

In late spring, like a small flock of migratory birds, this extraordinary trio would travel back to La Malcontenta where they resumed a way of life in which Venice was an inescapable reference point. It was a city that, for one reason or another, attracted many of the people whom they had met in Paris and London over the winter, as well as other intriguing characters whose company they found stimulating.

———

On August 20, 1933 Bertie dined in Venice with Serge Lifar. On this particular occasion he would also meet **Robert Byron**, an elegant twenty-eight-year-old, educated at Eton, who was "a gentleman, a scholar and an aesthete." The latter had chosen Venice, "the door to the Orient," as the starting point for a journey, which in due course would take him as far as Afghanistan.

Byron's travel journal (a "work of genius" which **Bruce Chatwin** regarded as a masterpiece of its genre)[60] opens with a striking phrase, indicative of the tone of the conversation at dinner that evening: "Bertie mentioned that all whales have syphilis."[61]

That Robert Byron visited Bertie on the banks of the Brenta two days later, together with Serge Lifar and other friends, was almost inevitable because Byron, whose knowledge of Palladian architecture was far from scholastic, was also genuinely interested in safeguarding the architectural heritage. It is worth noting in passing that this had prompted him to join the Georgian Group, an association that a little later became one of the most active anti-fascist organizations in the United Kingdom during the years leading up to the Second World War. Byron had unusually detailed knowledge of Byzantine architecture, as well as first-hand information on a matter of topical importance: the competition for the construction of the new Palace of the Soviets in Moscow.

From the report of Byron's visit to La Malcontenta in the opening pages of *The Road to Oxiana* we are given a taste of the fervor with which Bertie illustrated his choice of this house as the epicenter of his life: indeed, the very reason for his existence. In his diary, Byron records the words the owner spoke as the two men moved through the principal rooms whose proportions "are a mathematical paean," echoing an expression that Catherine frequently used.

Robert Byron, 1930s
Bruce Chatwin (photo: Lord Snowdon)

Where "[a]nother man would have filled them with so-called Italian furniture, antique-dealers' rubbish gilt ... Landsberg has had the furniture made of plain wood in the local village. Nothing is 'period' except the candles, which are necessary in the absence of electricity."[62]

As is clear from reading this account, Bertie asked his guests to come back inside the house before the sun set behind the Eugenean Hills, because he wanted them to admire the harmony of the space inside each room and the particular furnishings that he had devised, with Paul's help, precisely with the aim of not contaminating this architectural perfection.

Byron quickly went outside again. He offers no judgment of the south-facing façade or of the sides, limiting himself to noting the perplexities of a friend who could not understand the compositional techniques underlying its design ("people argue over the sides and affect to deplore the back"). Instead he focuses his attention on the main frontal façade. It "asks no opinion," he writes, adding, with an incisiveness that no architectural historian had achieved until then, "It is a precedent, a criterion. You can analyze it—nothing could be more lucid; but you cannot question it."

Standing in front of the villa in silence as the light faded, Byron waited with **Diana Cooper—Violet Lindsay**'s fascinating daughter (born when Violet was married to the Duke of Rutland), who had appeared on the front cover of *Time* a few years earlier in celebration of her physical beauty and extraordinary intellectual vivacity.[63]

"I stood with Diana," writes Byron in his journal, "on the lawn below the portico, as the glow before dusk defined for one moment more clearly every stage of the design. Europe could have bid me no fonder farewell than this triumphant affirmation of the European intellect." Darkness fell rapidly: "Inside, the candles were lit and Lifar danced."[64]

Robert Byron left Venice the next day at dawn, and journeyed to Trieste where he was due to embark. "The departure of this boat from Trieste was attended by scenes first performed in the Old Testament," he wrote on August 26. "A group of Jewish refugees from Germany were leaving for Palestine. There was both a venerable wonder-rabbi, whose orthodox ringlets and round beaver hat set the fashion for his disciples

Diana Cooper at the Lido, August 1932 (photo: Cecil Beaton)

down to the age of eight; on the other, a flashy group of
boys and girls in beach clothes, who stifled their emotions
by singing." This was 1933.

Engrossed in his own life, Bertie seems to have been
completely indifferent, almost extraneous, to the changing times;
he appeared to ignore these historic events, almost as if his
refusal to countenance them might banish them.

―――――

Parallel to this attitude towards the present, he also collected
slivers of the past, slivers whose unique, fragmentary nature
could serve as testament to the survival of a form of beauty,
even outside the context that had generated it and outside the
unity to which it had once belonged.

The surfaces of the house—the table tops, the low
bookcases—were absent-mindedly strewn with a fragment of
ancient plaster depicting a mysterious face, a marble calotte
adorned by a cluster of ringlets, a scrap of fabric embroidered
with running hares, a sheet bearing heavily inked lines, like
those from a woodcut, a musical instrument with an unusual
shape, a brass lamp with seven burners.

Each item had its own more or less evident identity and
charm. Each fragment served as a pretext, a hook to a story that
would lead the listener on unexpected journeys.

Only in front of the *menorah* did Bertie usually fall silent
as he waited to evaluate his companion's reaction. Otherwise,
he was all too ready to explain that the fragment of Pompeian
plaster was painted using a technique known as "fourth style";
that the face depicted on it was a theatrical mask; that the marble
curls may have adorned the head of a Hellenistic statue;
that the fabric was a piece of pile-on-pile velvet from the early
fifteenth century; that no undamaged woodcut by Mantegna
had yet been discovered; and that the *lira da braccio* (hand-held
lyre) resembled one depicted by Tintoretto in his paintings.

If the guest was cultured, or at least pretended to be
so, Bertie fell silent. On those occasions, the same fragments
served as rebuses or misleading clues, to test the visitor's
level of preparation.

However, a few years later, Bertie was disappointed to
lose a very young expert from Sotheby's at this game. The latter
came to visit La Malcontenta with Teddy Millington-Drake.

Bertie misjudged the risk of promising to give the young man
an item, if the latter could correctly guess what it was.
The fragment of sculpture lay, seemingly forgotten, between
the legs of a piece of furniture, on the ground floor. With all
the nonchalance of his youth, Bruce Chatwin instantly recognized the lump of grayish marble ("ten inches from the buttocks
and pelvis of a grayish marble kouros") as a fragment of
Attic sculpture dating from the sixth century B.C.; he promptly
picked it up off the floor, and took it away with him in a bag.[65]

Episodes of this kind amused Bertie, who found them
entertaining and stimulating, as by definition they improved
upon re-telling.

"He had the unusual advantage and strength of being
broadly clear, at the age of eleven or so, that his aim in life
would be the study and pursuit, the possession and adoration,
the constant contemplation and evaluation of beauty in
all its forms. And though tossed about by all, or more than the
normal flux of change, chance, passion and desire, he never lost
sight of that aim.

"From his earliest days he was a passionate looker, absorb-
ing form, light and shade, texture, pattern, color relationship:
noting and comparing. And judging by absolute standards,
without prejudice or predilection. His mind was singularly free
and open to new impressions and modes. His approach to all
works of art was sensual rather than intellectual and he became
scholarly chiefly from having 'read' and remembered an
immense quantity of works of art, rather than books about them:
though these, too, followed or accompanied. His reaction to
a work of art was spontaneous and immediate, though he might
return to it for a lifetime of study and observation."

Claud Phillimore (who would write these words in 1972,
a few years after Bertie's death) arrived at La Malcontenta—
where those gaudily feathered hens, which had charmed Catherine in Rome, were still roaming around—one day in October,
again in 1933.

———

This supremely elegant twenty-two-year-old was the son of
Godfrey Walter, 2nd Baron Phillimore. Claud, who was now
studying architecture at Trinity College, Cambridge, was
accompanied by his stepmother, **Marion Phillimore** (formerly

Bryce; Dorothy Barbara Balfour Haig, his mother, had drowned in the Thames many years earlier while attempting to save her firstborn son). As well as visiting Venice, appreciating the city's beauty and the works of art conserved in its museums, Claud had also planned a trip to Padua. He followed—in reverse order—the same itinerary that Bertie and Catherine had chosen on their way to Venice. He boarded a vaporetto at the Zattere, and on arriving at Fusina, he took the *tramvia* along the north bank of the Riviera.

When he caught sight of the Palladian villa on the other side of the watercourse, Claud promptly left the train, followed by Marion, not caring that this stop was not included on his itinerary. He hastened impatiently towards the austere façade, embellished by the central portico in hexastyle Ionic order. He stood, filled with emotion, in front of the building, which still seemed to be enveloped in an atmosphere of solitude. Then he walked down the short stretch of road—the one along which Bertie and Catherine had also approached the palace for the first time. Like them, Claud entered through a half-open door.

Before him were the perfectly proportioned spaces, rooms whose elegant atmosphere was almost tangible; he was overcome by a wave of emotion that he could still vividly recall years later. A woman walked to meet him as he entered the large central hall: "No longer young, but of great beauty, with a mass of red hair swept back from clear-cut, classic features and with topaz eyes glinting with green and golden lights. She was dressed in a rough overall loosely pinned together by a magnificent emerald brooch." Catherine did not usually expect visitors at this time of day. "'How do you do?' she said in a warm and deeply attractive voice, broken by a slight French accent 'full of the warm south': 'How do you do? I don't like visitors'."

Some time passed—half an hour, or even an hour—before Bertie also appeared, under the portico: "A man in his forties, stout, but finely built, with distinguished features and warm (if the term can be used of such a color) expressive eyes of a blue almost aquamarine."

Bertie Landsberg, Marion Phillimore, and Claud Phillimore at La Malcontenta

Claud's elegance and graceful smile prompted Bertie to
recount, with his usual fervor, the various stages of the enterprise as they wandered through each of the ground floor
rooms, and then spent even longer on the *piano nobile*. He took
Claud up the narrow staircase that led to that unsuspected,
almost secret world above the fresco cycle ideally depicted
on the ceiling of the *piano nobile*: the universe that lay above
the clouds on which Astraea, the virgin goddess, had lingered
before she finally left the earth.

Claud was entranced by Bertie's "remarkable and
rarely gifted personality." This marked the start of an exchange
of thoughts and feelings between the two men, as described
by Claud many years later, after the passage of time had
distilled the essence of this youthful experience.

"And then how to estimate what he gave out in generous,
compassionate human sympathy and understanding? And
to remember the riches of his conversation! He had a mind so
stored with sensitive knowledge, observation, and distilled
experience, that the most casual, chance remark would often
release a flood of thoughtful comparison, embroidery and
reminiscence which would leave one gasping at so rich a return
on so paltry an investment. The enthralling torrent of words
would flow, eager, apt, and illuminating, interrupted by warm,
infectious laughter and more than Jamesian parentheses—
on the landing of the stairs, over an unceasingly renewed lather
while shaving, at ease in the beautiful rooms, or across the
table over delicious and prolonged feasts in the shade of the
acacia grove at Malcontenta. Conversation shared with and
taken up by so many people who represented all that was most
vital and creative in the artistic world of many countries."

"Years later," Claud wrote, "I learned that the owner of
all these wonders had gone the next day to his lawyer in Venice
and made his will, leaving them all to me."

———

That this visit to La Malcontenta was a life-changing event
for Claud was remarked on by his step-sister, **Amaryllis Bryce**,
the member of his family with whom Claud had a greater
understanding than with his other relatives. She immediately
asked him about the *palazzo*, a question that Claud, replying
to her from Cambridge on a cold day in December or possibly

January, avoided by stating, "I would have to draw thirty-two windows, incredibly precisely, in order to show it to you."

"I thought I would never see them again, Catherine and Bertie," Claud continued, in an attempt to stave off Amaryllis' curiosity. "Then they re-appeared here [in London], and by some miracle they remembered that I live here [in Cambridge] and they invited me to dinner."

As on previous occasions, Claud began his letter describing Catherine, rather than Bertie. His "fascinating new friend" has red hair, that color you only see in shells. Someone (perhaps Claud himself?) wrote a poem about her: "the perfect Baroness was there/with coral in her Titianesque hair." Claud went on: "she is intelligent, lively and amusing, she paints very well—portraits, in particular—and she's full of interesting ideas about architecture and decoration. She has six names, all different and exotic." In *Down the Garden Path*, **Beverley Nichols** dedicates the book "To Marie Rose Antoinette Catherine de Robert d'Aqueria Rochegude d'Erlanger whose charms are as gay and numerous as her names."[66]

"She has a beautiful house filled with precious things: wall tapestries and gilded wallpaper; a long room in which the dancers from the *Russian Ballets* have performed. She owns all of Byron's things, and hundreds of rare shells. The most fascinating room is the sitting-room where she lives and works. The windows look out over Green Park and Buckingham Palace, and the walls are filled with portraits painted by her: they are all magnificent, pale and shell-colored. There are piles of books, photographs, shells and other things all over the floor, and on the chairs. Everything is in perfect confusion."

In this account—which is of the same tenor as the one Claud would write a few decades later, recalling his first visit to La Malcontenta—Bertie appears at a later stage. In the meantime the scene has moved from Catherine's house to the Ritz, the hotel that Bertie gave as his London address when he did not want to reveal that he was living at the Baroness's residence.

When Bertie ("a Brazilian who is the owner of La Malcontenta") does arrive, he is in the company of "a very charming and intelligent Egyptian." Claud then goes on to describe two particularly distinctive figures entering the hotel lobby: "another student who was twenty-foot tall," whom Catherine invited to lunch in spite of never having met him before, and immediately afterwards, in the *lounge*, a traveling salesman wearing a pepper and salt suit and a bow tie.

The latter butted in—as Claud recounts—interrupting a conversation on the subject of religion in which "everyone spoke simultaneously at the tops of their voices about different things, and never answered anyone else's questions."

At the end of the evening, Claud returned to Cambridge, to the house he shared with **Eric Duncannon**,[67] taking with him three gifts: "four meters of *chintz* (designed by Catherine), a book on La Malcontenta, a gift from Bertie, and a crystal droplet from a chandelier which—if you look through it—transforms the world into a magical place, filled with geometric shapes."

"Life is very odd," he concluded; and at this point he finally added a sketch of the Palace, which is a sort of montage, a combination of the drawing in Palladio's treatise and a photographic view that was in circulation at the time. In closing, he passed the buck to his step-sister by adding, "Let me know what you think about all this."

———

Claud's arrival at La Malcontenta—as well as changing, in a wholly unexpected manner, the fate of the *palazzo*—was, to some extent, also a sign of the changes underway in that special sort of bond that had formed almost a decade earlier between Bertie, Catherine, and Paul (this had become the sequence now official).

It was as if the intimacy that united them first became complicity and then started to evaporate before they themselves were able to realize it.

When Bertie did not spend the day in Venice, he explored the plain west of the lagoon in a quest for excitement and pleasure that was, to some extent, a therapeutic exercise. He would summon a driver—one from the many handsome youths who arrived at the palace to offer their services—and would be driven to a particular hillside. There he would enter a monastery, explore a park, visit a ceramics workshop, and return a visit, stopping at a villa for lunch. He observed everything carefully: the mortar used in a medieval brick wall, the composition of a Venetian terrazzo floor, or the metal fittings of an old window, which had somehow survived in a crumbling building.

F.E.N. ("Eric") Ponsonby, Viscount Duncannon, later Earl of Bessborough, 1933 (t.l.)
Claud Phillimore, at Little Trinity, Cambridge 1933 (t.r.); staying with Viscount
Duncannon at Stratton House, 1934 (b.l.)
Claud Phillimore, Catherine d'Erlanger and "Baba" at Stratton House, 1934 (b.r.)

Catherine d'Erlanger with her bibelots, Piccadilly House, London 1930
(t.l., photo: Cecil Beaton)
The "Casa Rosa" on the Riva degli Schiavoni, dining room, 1933
(r., photo: Mario Giacomelli)
Norah Lindsay (b.l.)

Returning home in the evening, having visited another Palladian *fabbrica*, he would stand in the yard of the *barchessa* looking towards the house to which his life was by now inextricably whispering in a satisfied tone, "but mine is the most beautiful."

When he felt no desire to go out, he rose later than usual and dressed in an ample silk dressing gown. He felt no qualms about going out into the garden dressed in this showy attire and would summon Teodato if the latter had failed, in Bertie's opinion, to give sufficient water to the large terracotta vases containing the lemon trees.

Otherwise, he would slowly open a brocade-covered box and choose a record. Then, turning on the gramophone—the type with an articulated arm and needle—he would stretch out on a divan in the crossings of the central hall. The fresco decoration and the music immediately blended and merged as Rossini's notes swirled around the figures by Zelotti, enveloping them in sound. When silence finally returned, Bertie stood up slowly (he suffered from a weak heart) and started to wander through the rooms, barefoot. Engrossed, he wanted to feel the sensation through the soles of his feet on a floor—with its antique *pastellone* tiles—which was as soft as the well-oiled leather of a saddle, and also slightly undulating. He sought a physical sensation, a perception that would not prompt a Proustian-type memory, nor hope. It was purely hedonistic. Then he sat down with a book and continued to read, surrounded by books, until the light faded as the sun set.

Catherine was often away. She needed to feel the buzz of city life around her, to meet people, walk into a shop—best of all, a bric-a-brac shop—or be invited to dinner by a passing friend, or even to invite a complete stranger. She needed these random encounters.

She bought a new house on Riva degli Schiavoni, from whose windows, flooded with light from the south, she could see the church of San Giorgio, le Zittelle, and the Redentore. Even here, there was a little bit of Palladio. She called this new residence the "pink house," a joking reference to the *Palais Rose* that had been Robert de Montesquiou's Parisian base. She furnished it with her usual flair, making it all beauty and colors, to use the words of **Norah Lindsay** who sent this description to her sisters: "her fascinating dining room of small tables—all round the walls—which are in tableau of pearl shells, and old Venetian mirrors set into grass green marbled walls— is one of the prettiest rooms I've even seen."[68]

However long she stayed in Venice, Catherine neither forgot nor neglected Bertie. She made sure to board the vaporetto to Fusina, from where she took the train to Malcontenta. Having been informed of her arrival, Bertie would climb into the *sandolo* (a boat), which he kept moored in the inlet, and although he had not yet mastered the art of rowing (and never would) he collected her from the station on the opposite bank of the Riviera. Then he took her home, without having to go around through the village.

———

Catherine immediately sprang into action as soon as she disembarked. She summoned the tenant farmer to report on the progress of the orchard of peach trees, which she had had planted on land not required by Bertie for the garden. She also checked the henhouse, oversaw the management of the house, and organized the meals. Yet the question of menus was not of particular concern: meals at Bertie's house were almost always frugal (it was common knowledge in the village that when the parish priest was invited to dinner, as happened with ritual regularity each year, his *perpetua* [housekeeper] was ordered to prepare a large dish of pasta as soon as he returned to the *canonica*). Instead, what Catherine had to choose was the place where the lunch or dinner would be served. If they dined *al fresco,* she would arrange for heavy jute cloths to be pulled out of the wooden chest where they were usually stored. The guests would then be invited to wrap these cloths around their legs in order to protect themselves from the mosquitoes, which, this close to the Riviera, were particularly vicious at certain times of the year. If, on the other hand, she decided to have the table prepared inside the portico, she would hang old, rust-colored sails from a *bragozzo* (fishing boat) to the nails that, in the past, had been used to hold *appliques* (torches) on the columns. (Bertie had thought up this solution in order to be able to move around freely, naked, in the portico, on sultry summer days, while waiting for relief from the cool evening breeze.) The sails served to protect the diners from the view of passers-by on the towpath.

Paul at Rue de Montauban

When they were alone, Bertie and Catherine swapped opinions of the people they had met, and exchanged the names of new visitors to Venice whom they would like to get to know. They also planned trips. In some corner of their minds, they shared a fascination for the "elsewhere." Both dreamed, almost always, of the Orient, and sometimes they imagined following in Robert Byron's footsteps.

Bertie, who had read *Les Orientales*, shared the idea that the Jews, Turks, Arabs, Persians and Spanish were also oriental, since, as Victor Hugo states in the preface to that poem, "Spain is still the Orient; Spain is half African, and Africa is half Asian."[69]

Catherine, who was less abstract than Bertie in her way of thinking, wondered whether Rodolphe, her husband's brother, might not have been right. Having decided to leave London and Paris, and to abandon business and society life, he had built a large house on a cliff with a breath-taking view of the Gulf of Tunis, and here, surrounded by every imaginable comfort, he spent his time cultivating the pleasures that the Arab civilization had refined to a surprising degree over the centuries.

Paul's absence from La Malcontenta during these summer days was palpable. It was impossible even to imagine that, inclined as he was to escape any noise or voice, he might be upstairs in the east room, his favorite retreat, intent on preparing a drawing. Moreover, it was no longer the adventure in Neuilly that distracted him from the banks of the Brenta, because Arturo-José had now embarked on a succession of foreign trips, funded by the large resources to which he now had access.

Paul had met an extraordinary man who had assimilated Marcel Proust's philosophy, almost as if he had lived alongside him for years (whereas in truth he had never met him). This individual, **Jean-Michel Frank**, had successfully forged his life into that extremely rare combination of asceticism and dandyism, which had made him a celebrity in the most sophisticated Parisian circles.

It seems likely that Paul had met Jean-Michel Frank at the house of **Eugenia Errazuriz**, Arturo-José's aunt. Among the ladies who moved in the city's most exclusive circles, she was the one who fervently supported the theory that furnishing is an art, achieved by removing everything that can be removed from a house, and reducing everything—even the form of a piece of furniture—to its essential qualities.

In addition to the stimulus he received from the avant-garde movements, which enlivened the cultural scene in Paris during these years, it was this lesson that had helped Jean-Michel to discover his vocation as a decorator. Moreover, his considerable personal fortune had allowed him to enter into collaboration with **Adolphe Chanaux**'s studio in the Rue de Montauban—which could realize his designs for supremely elegant objects using the rarest of materials, like ivory or shagreen, or extremely poor materials like straw, whose aesthetic qualities were enhanced using special techniques performed by highly qualified craftsmen.

However, by meeting Frank, Paul was able, miraculously, to find a middle way between the excesses resulting from Arturo-José's exorbitant wealth and the constraints imposed by Bertie's limited finances. The paucity of funds meant that Bertie was forced to resort to using old carriage springs as torch holders, or to embellish firedogs made from scrap iron with the knobs from antique banisters.

It mattered little that some commented, ironically, that Frank's furniture represented "a sort of poverty that not many in the world could afford." It offered a primary, although perhaps not the only, channel that allowed him, and those who wanted to follow his example, to confront modernity without giving way to any type of functionalism.

One need only look at the photo of Paul with **Diego Giacometti**, Adolphe Chanaux (the partner of **Jean-Michel Frank**), **Christian Bérard** (a friend who frequently stayed at La Malcontenta), **Emilio Terry**, Jean-Michel Frank and **Alberto Giacometti**, to see how gratified Paul was—although, even now, he never renounced his self-imposed role as the master of composure—at being closer to the Surrealists, to the Groupe des Six, to Aragon, to Eluard, to René Crével, and to the aristocratic circles—above all the one surrounding Vicomte Charles de Noailles—than he would have been if he had remained at La Malcontenta, hidden away in his room.

———

At La Malcontenta

Bertie did not follow Paul on his chosen path; he could not follow him, just as he could not follow Catherine in her movements between London, Paris, and the other centers where, at agreed moments, European high society would convene. He left La Malcontenta on rare occasions, and only during the summer. It had to be for a specific reason, such as attending Claud's sister's wedding, where, after the ceremony, a dinner was held under the cover of a large marquee in blue cellophane. This episode was recorded by Catherine's old friend, the one who had seen Bertie dressed as a Roman centurion at the grand party given by Andrea di Robilant in Palazzo Mocenigo.

Norah Lindsay—who in the meantime had become a famous garden designer—had already developed a sincere friendship with Bertie whom she regarded as "cultivated and amorous." She almost seemed protective towards him. She understood his hesitations and was willing to tolerate the slight awkwardness he demonstrated in day-to-day life. Prompted by these feelings, she regularly stayed in the "glorious palazzo" on the banks of the Brenta whenever she came to Venice, even if she found it annoying that the draft—passing straight through the ineffective shutters—blew out the candle in her bedroom when she wanted to stay up late in order to write her letters. However, in spite of these discomforts (and the discovery of a scorpion menacingly close to her bed), she even paid for her lodging in order to help cover the household expenses, which were always more than the landlord's finances could afford.

The stream of visitors to the *palazzo* continued to be a regular feature, even during these years; indeed, after so many seasons, it had become almost a ritual procedure. These visitors were perhaps also a necessity for a man who took refuge in the hope, though without too many illusions, that a cosmopolis existed: a sort of network of elect, or at least select, individuals who, in some way or other, represented the world (even if, by now, as Bertie himself acknowledged, they were no longer responsible for its outcome).

Each new encounter offered Bertie an occasion to entrance his listener with the range of his knowledge and with the art of entertaining—not to say seducing—in which he

In Jean-Michel Frank's boutique, 1935, top: Paul Rodocanachi, Diego Giacometti,
Adolphe Chanaux, Emilio Terry, Jean-Michel Frank, Christian Bérard and
Alberto Giacometti; bottom: Alberto Giacometti, Jean-Michel Frank, Emilio Terry,
Paul Rodocanachi, Christian Bérard, Adolphe Chanaux, Diego Giacometti
(from left to right, photos: François Kollar)

Christian Bérard at La Malcontenta, 1930 (photo: Boris Kochno)

Pablo Picasso, *Boris Kochno*, 1921
Christian Bérard in the central hall of La Malcontenta, 1930 (photo: Boris Kochno)

was extremely well versed. What was more, it meant that he could gratify that curiosity which continued to be a key trait of his personality. Each guest opened up a whole world for him to explore, sometimes revealing unexpected surprises.

_____

It was in this spirit that Bertie welcomed **Anthony Blunt**, a Fellow of Trinity College, Cambridge, and, without hesitating, persuaded him to accept Claud as one of his pupils, given that the latter had not yet finished his studies there.

But it was not only an interest in Renaissance art and architecture that led the young Anthony Blunt to Venice in 1934, and from Venice to La Malcontenta. Knowing that Bertie knew Giuseppe Volpi, Blunt tried to discover whether Bertie had any idea what had prompted the multi-talented business-man to promote a meeting between Hitler and Mussolini, and to do everything he could to ensure that it should take place in Venice. Indeed, at that moment, there was no political reason that could justify a rapprochement between the two heads of state given that Mussolini was determined to oppose any idea of German rearmament, condemned the interference of the Nazi regime in Austrian politics, and was not willing to accept any racist theory.

When the conversation drifted onto this subject, Bertie— who was only vaguely aware of the German Chancellor's imminent visit—could not have imagined for one instant what no one in Europe would know for many years yet: namely, that Anthony Blunt, his brilliant visitor, the Cambridge scholar soon to be appointed Surveyor of the King's Pictures, was already working for the Soviet Secret Service. It seems likely that it was for intelligence purposes that Blunt returned to Venice, and therefore to La Malcontenta, in 1936, when the political union between Fascism and Nazism was achieved.

It must have been with amazement rather than alarm that Bertie, a few weeks later, watched the procession of cars traveling towards Stra, along the road flanking the Riviera, on the bank opposite his house. They were escorting Hitler to the sumptuous villa, built by the Pisanis at the end of the eighteenth century, where Mussolini awaited him.

If both Catherine and Paul arrived at La Malcontenta in the summer of 1934, it was not out of political interest, but because

this year was also filled with all the events which Giuseppe
Volpi had planned and organized in order to transform Venice
into "the Geneva of the arts."

As well as the Film Festival, Volpi had decided to set up
a Theater Festival; he also organized a conference on the *Institut International de Coopération Intellectuelle,* which would
be held inside the halls of the Doge's Palace, an Electro-Radio-
Biology Congress chaired by **Guglielmo Marconi,** and—
alongside events of this kind—a series of sporting events and
social engagements to be held on the waters of the lagoon
itself, on the beaches of the Lido, in the grand hotels which
Volpi owned, and in those Venetian palaces which were still
"furnished" (*montati*) (including the one inhabited by Annina
Morosini, of course).

Bertie's *palazzo* was also indirectly involved in these
events, if for no other reason than that it obliged guests wishing
to visit it to cross the construction which Volpi had promoted
and of which he was particularly proud: the bridge across the
lagoon, which had been finished a few months earlier.

Guglielmo Marconi also came to La Malcontenta.
To commemorate the visit—and perhaps to record the Fascist
regime's use of the Nobel laureate for propaganda—Bertie
glued an image of Marconi in his pompous uniform as Acca-
demico d'Italia in the visitors' book.

———

Quite different in nature—and therefore not at all formal—
was the welcome reserved for Le Corbusier, by then a famous
architect. It had surprised the intellectuals who were taking
part in the *Entretien,* a symposium being held in the Doge's
Palace to exalt the unrepeatable uniqueness of the city of Venice,
and to celebrate the gondola as an exemplary expression of
functionality and incomparable proof of the aesthetic excellence
that can be achieved through standardization.

The meeting was arranged by **Sir Eric Maclagan,** a friend
of Bertie's, who, as director of the Victoria and Albert Museum,
had also been involved in the realization of the *Entretien* organized by the *Institut International de Coopération Intellectuelle.*

Le Corbusier was drawn to La Malcontenta by his continued interest in Palladian architecture, but other matters also
prompted him to visit. He knew that Bertie, who was Brazilian

by birth (and sometimes jokingly introduced himself as a member of the Brazilian diplomatic corps), intended, on the same occasion, to invite a Brazilian diplomat—the commercial attaché at The Hague. The latter, **Caio de Mello Franco**, had good relations with the government authorities of Brazil and would therefore be well placed to help Le Corbusier resume the contacts he needed to pursue, with some likelihood of success, his dream of realizing the grandiose projects, which he had conceived on his first visit to South America.

Le Corbusier knew, too, that Catherine could easily arrange a meeting with Giuseppe Volpi and that she was also the right person, thanks to her enterprising character, to act as the go-between for the project which dominated his thoughts on his arrival in Venice: to persuade Volpi to abandon the program (which Le Corbusier judged to be "criminal") of building a "garden city" behind the industrial port, and instead to embark on the construction of a new kind of urban settlement, using Le Corbusier's design.[70]

In this climate, a mood of excitement spread through the small group of people gathered in the rooms of the Palladian building. Catherine could not restrain her extrovert and impulsive temperament; she wanted to paint a portrait of Le Corbusier and also to convince him, without delay, to design a project for an aquarium in Venice.[71] Caio de Mello Franco, who was a notable poet as well as a reliable and proficient diplomat,[72] offered to support Le Corbusier's approaches to the Brazilian government, and in the meantime continued to film those present in the room.[73]

Le Corbusier—who had the self-assurance to manage his fame—neatly sidestepped Catherine's insistence, stating, as he later recalled, that "aquariums are often natural horror museums."[74] Instead he tried to persuade her to commission him to build a house in Venice, in the hope that he could therefore leave a trace of himself in a city that he described as "a unique phenomenon, in its current state of conservation, of total harmony, integral purity and unity of civilisation."[75] To Mello Franco, who particularly interested him, he promised to give one of the books he had written, as well as two sketches which he had made in 1929, when he had formulated his visionary proposals for the urban redefinition of Rio de Janeiro.[76]

140

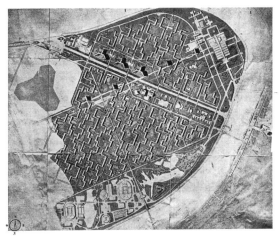

Le Corbusier speaks in the Doge's Palace during the symposium *Art and State* in
Venice in 1934
Le Corbusier, city planning for the left bank of the Escaut, Antwerp, general plan, 1933

Catherine d'Erlanger, letter to
Le Corbusier, August 28, 1934

"[…] Here's an idea that's been in my mind
for a long time. I would like there to be an
aquarium in Venice. It would be so beautiful
with the fish from the Adriatic.
The interior would be like the one in
London. Do you know it? Polished black
and just luminous tanks filled with aquatic
things.
But the exterior … well, that's where your
flair would be evident.
Would you like to think about it? It would
be wonderful to have one of your designs in
Venice—built using beautiful local materials,
of course. Istrian stone, glass, etc.
We would have to ensure that the city
accepted your project, and also find the
money. …

What do you think? There would
be no problem about getting the water.
There's already a solution for that.
You promised me a book with some of
photos of you. Don't forget.
Au revoir. I would like to paint your
portrait one day.
Opposite me, San Giorgio is looking
across and sending you best wishes through
Palladio.
Me too. […]"

142

Le Corbusier, 1930s

LE CORBUSIER
&
P.

PARIS, le 12 Septembre 1934

Baronne d'ERLANGER
Casa Rosa
Riva Schiavone
VENISE

Chère Madame et Amie,

J'ai reçu à la mer votre gentille lettre du 26 Août.
Si je suis occupé d'autres affaires, les casiers que j'ai dans la tête
conservent tout de même ce que j'ai ressenti à Venise tout particulièrement.
Par conséquent, je ne suis pas près d'abandonner les souvenirs vénitiens.

Votre lettre contient des choses positives : la première, c'est l'idée de construire à Venise un aquarium. Evidemment cette
idée m'intéresse beaucoup. Je connais l'aquarium de Londres que le directeur même du Jardin Zoologique m'a fait visiter à la Pentecôte. C'est très
intéressant de faire un aquarium, je ne demande pas mieux. Cela me fera
même un très grand plaisir. La difficulté est de faire de l'architecture
aussi belle que certains des poissons de la mer Adriatique (je ne dis pas
tous, car les aquariums sont souvent le Musée des horreurs naturelles, au
point de vue humain bien entendu.). Vous voici donc fixée pour l'aquarium : d'accord.

Mais ce qui m'intéresserait beaucoup plus et je vous
le disais sauf erreur dans ma lettre, ce serait d'essayer à Venise de
faire une maison moderne (une maison ordinaire, la maison d'un honnête
homme) en accord avec les splendeurs de l'architecture du passé. Et par
splendeur j'entends tout autant la maison modeste que le Palais. Et ma
maison d'honnête homme peut être tout aussi bien pour personne riche ou
pas riche. La question n'est pas là, la question est de trouver une harmonie entre aujourd'hui et hier et cela tout simplement par une unité dic-
tée par les lieux et par la destination, tout en employant les techniques
d'aujourd'hui avec, si possible, autant de brio que les Vénitiens d'autre-
fois ont employé les techniques les plus "à la page" de leur temps. Plus
je voyage, plus je mesure que c'est l'esprit contemporain qui constitue,
générations après générations, la chaîne de la parenté, l'harmonie humaine,
et l'unité fondamentale. Tout regard en arrière crée un mensonge et un
hiatus.

Conclusion : j'aimerais infiniment pouvoir faire
cette chose-là. C'est une gageure en face de la splendeur de la ville de
Venise.

Le second point dont m'entretient votre lettre est
une chose bien importante et qui me serait très chère, c'est le contact à
F
LC

Le Corbusier, letter to Catherine d'Erlanger, September 12, 1934

"[…] Your letter contains positive news: the first is the idea of building an aquarium in Venice. Of course, I would be very interested. I know the London aquarium which the director of the Zoo himself took me to visit at Pentecost. It would be very interesting to do an aquarium, I couldn't think of anything better. It will also give me great pleasure. The difficulty would be to design a building as beautiful as some of the fish in the Adriatic (I won't say all of them because aquariums often resemble a museum of natural horrors, from the human point of view, of course). So you're resolved on the aquarium: I agree. […]"

PARIS, le 12 Septembre 1934

prendre avec le Comte VOLPI au sujet de la ville d'habitation de la nouvelle Venise industrielle. Vous m'encouragez à intervenir. Lorsque
j'étais à Venise, j'étais plein de feu et d'indignation aussi, et je sen-
tais de mon devoir de renseigner un homme de la valeur du Comte VOLPI sur
l'état actuel des idées et des moyens en matière d'habitation. Les dis-
tances sont homicides, on finit par être désarticulé, mais je ferai par-
venir au Comte VOLPI une note et des documents. La seule chose qui m'in-
quiète, c'est qu'il n'ait pas le temps de lire ces derniers et que mon
intervention soit de ce fait de la nature d'une piqûre de moustique, et
rien de plus.

L'Italie se réveille formidablement, l'architecture
et l'urbanisme y éclatent partout. L'accueil qu'on m'a fait à Rome et
à Milan est tel que je puis, sans forfanterie, admettre une part de la
paternité dans cette renaissance italienne (comme le mot est joli !). Si
le Comte VOLPI voulait bien, comme vous le dites, faire appel à des gens
venus de tout le monde, et me charger de lui expliquer quelles applica-
tions peut être faite à Venise de la révolution architecturale et urbanis-
tique dans le domaine de l'habitation, j'en serais charmé. Je suis arrivé
à un âge où l'on commence presque à se lasser de toujours frapper à la
porte des autres et où l'on aimerait bien que, de temps en temps, on
vienne vous appeler. Je laisse cette question entre vos mains, je sais
qu'elle ne pourrait trouver de meilleure messagère et vous seriez gentille
de me faire savoir, lorsque l'occasion s'en sera présentée, ce que je
dois faire dans cette affaire relative à la ville d'habitation de la
Venise industrielle.

Vous me réclamez le numéro spécial de l'Architecture
d'Aujourd'hui, je vous le fais envoyer demain. Vous pourrez, entre autres,
lire le rapport concernant l'urbanisation de la nouvelle ville d'Anvers
(cas analogue, en plus grand, à celui de la Venise industrielle). Un rapport
c'est toujours ennuyeux, mais les faits qui sont évoqués dans celui-ci
constituent un poème des Temps Modernes. Je le dis en toute sérénité.

Je vous dicte cette lettre dans mon bureau, vous
imaginez bien que l'atmosphère n'est plus ici à la contemplation des
couchers de soleil sur St-Georges Majeur, vous me pardonnerez d'être
devenu un vilain homme d'affaires.

Croyez, chère Madame et amie, à mon meilleur souvenir.

In the short interval between these two "professional" episodes (which would prompt Le Corbusier to apologize to Catherine in case his behavior had seemed that of a "vilain homme d'affaire"("a rude businessman"), Bertie took Le Corbusier on a tour of the rooms, highlighting that synthesis created in them through the fusion of architecture and painting.

The visit remained firmly impressed in Le Corbusier's mind. A few months later a clear memory of it came to mind, when all talk of the residential development behind the industrial port, of the aquarium, and even of the house that Le Corbusier had intended to build in Venice, had evaporated. Instead he was on a liner, crossing the Atlantic.[77]

———

Le Corbusier was returning from Rio de Janeiro where, thanks to the support of Caio de Mello Franco, he had been called by the Brazilian government and had inspired the outline of a project for a new Ministry of Culture and a plan to build the university campus. By chance Bertie was on the same boat, on his way back to Europe after visiting his relatives, who lived in Petropolis.[78] Le Corbusier was surprised and at the same time pleased by this chance meeting with "the fortunate owner of one of Palladio's most important creations": an "architecture of great purity," he wrote, which continues to give profound joy to this "old friend."[79]

He was so enthused by this exchange of ideas with the "garçon" (as he teasingly called Bertie) that he felt a growing desire—almost an impulse—to create a monument that would evoke the model of La Malcontenta: a "villa" in which architecture and painting would merge in absolute synthesis to form a monument blending the aspirations of an entire century. He was certain that he could involve the great artists who had trained in the same cultural climate as he had also grown up in; they—and he named Léger, Picasso, Braque, Lipchitz, Brancusi, and Laurens—would, he hoped, be keen to join him in carrying out this operation.[80]

But it was not only the Palladian *fabbrica* in itself that fired his imagination: it was also the way it was run by its owner. Indeed, Le Corbusier was merely describing Bertie's own habits when he said that the owner of the villa he planned to build, inspired by the model of Palladio's La Malcontenta, could live in a small house beside it, if the resulting building was not comfortable enough for everyday life.

Le Corbusier was so excited by this idea that he planned to immediately discuss his idea with his friends Soby and Hitchcock, so they could help him to find a sponsor who could finance the construction. He was then overcome by anxiety when he realized that he might not have enough time to complete the work. "In five years it will be too late and in ten ... we'll all be dead," he wrote to **Everett Austin** (a journalist he was confident to attract the attention, and therefore the financial support, of the Museum of Modern Art).[81]

It was possibly the enthusiasm of Bertie's approach and the charisma he exerted over those he met which attracted the attention of a young scholar, who was still in his early thirties. Until 1932 this young man had worked alongside the Director of the Hertziana Library in Rome, compiling a bibliography of works on Michelangelo Buonarroti; after moving to London in 1933, he had then dedicated a further two years to a study of Michelangelo's architecture.

———

Bertie turned to **Rudolf Wittkower** for an opinion on the frescos depicting the Giants, which, according to Ovid's tale, were destroyed by Jupiter as a punishment for having dared to climb Olympus. Bertie wanted to discover whether these frescos were the work of **Battista Franco**, an artist who had visited Rome where he had the opportunity to learn directly from Michelangelo.[82]

But there were also other matters that interested Bertie and Rudolf Wittkower—so much so that the latter, writing from Villa Coccini where he was staying with his wife, hoped to have time for further discussion: "If thereafter you would find me an opportunity of discussing things of common interest to both you and me, I shall be extremely glad to see you."[83]

When they met at La Malcontenta, Bertie had shared a number of reflections with his young visitor. In the same way as he had done with Le Corbusier, he engaged in conversation on topics varying from Palladio's architectural legacy (his architectural opus, from the public buildings and palaces to the villas and churches) to the principles that dictated the composition of his projects, to the harmonic proportions

PARIS - 35 rue de Sèvres - VI°

le 27 Juillet 1939

E2 14

Monsieur Rex MARTIENSSEN
2, Athlone Road
Parkview
JOHANNESBURG

Mon cher Martienssen,

Votre ami, Mr John Fassler qui m'a commandé le tableau m'a écrit récemment en me disant qu'il serait heureux de me recevoir si j'allais une fois à Johannesburg.

Johannesburg me paraissait être exactement au bout du monde, au milieu des lions et des nègres, c'est-à-dire inaccessible. Or, l'autre jour, j'ai déjeuné à Zürich avec un grand homme d'affaires qui m'a dit le plus grand bien possible de Johannesburg et des habitants de Johannesburg, en particulier, affirmant que vous êtes des gentlemen exceptionnels et que c'est un pays du plus haut intérêt. Il m'a engagé absolument à partir, en prenant l'avion d'Imperial Airways.

Toutcela est très joli et très tentant, mais avec mes poches vides, cela va très mal. Réfléchissant à la question, je m'imagine éventuellement ceci : ne pourriez-vous pas trouver à Johannesburg un mécène qui désire se faire faire une villa exceptionnellement soignée et dont j'établirais les plans et que je ferais exécuter par vous et vos amis. On pourrait même, étant donné l'excellent état d'esprit qui règne chez vous, faire une démonstration extraordinaire d'art moderne par de la peinture (fresque ou agrandissements photographiques, etc...). Je serais certain même d'avoir la collaboration de quelques-uns de mes meilleurs amis, des meilleurs artistes existants.

A ce sujet, je tiens le raisonnement que j'ai tenté de faire admettre, en 1936, sur le bateau, à l'un des plus riches planteurs de café du Brésil. Je lui disais : il serait possible à tout homme ayant une somme pas nécessairement élevée de construire une villa dans l'esprit des villas de Palladio, à la Renaissance, avec moi comme architecte et mes amis comme peintres et sculpteurs - la consigne étant de faire ce qu'il y a de plus parfaitement imaginable. Ce propriétaire pourrait même habiter dans une autre maison à lui, à côté, mais il aurait une espèce de joyaux du XX° siècle qui serait connu universellement et qui permettrait à ceux de ma génération (passé 50 ans) et qui représentent l'une des périodes les plus héroïques de cette période qui certainement ne se trouvera pas. Le point de départ de ma proposition était celle-ci : c'est qu'il est exceptionnel de pouvoir trouver des artistes de cinquante ans qui ont conservé leur pleine confiance mutuelle et qui sont préparés pour une tâche architecturale et monumentale par trente années de luttes antérieures.

J'ajouterai même que celui qui m'avait donné l'idée de cette proposition était mon ami Landsberg qui est le propriétaire de la villa "Malcontenta" de Palladio, à Mestres, près Venise, villa qui lui donne des joies profondes puisqu'elle est d'une architecture très pure et qu'elle est décorée par Véronèse et ses élèves. C'est lui qui estimait que nous aussi, en 1939, 1940, nous aurions quelque chose à dire.

Pourquoi pas ?

Je laisse ce sujet à votre méditation. Avec de la foi, on peut soulever des montagnes...

Bien cordialement à vous et à tous vos amis.

Le Corbusier, letter to Rex
Martienssen, July 27, 1939

"[…] it would be possible for anyone with money, not necessarily a large amount, to build a villa in the spirit of those built by Palladio, in the Renaissance style, with myself as the architect and my friends as painters and sculptors.... Some friends who were there at the time thought it was a great idea. I would also add that the person who gave me the idea was my friend, Landsberg, who owns the Palladian villa "Malcontenta," at Mestre, near Venice, a villa that gives him immense joy. […]"

ther case are they
.tionship with the
wall.
: base is not con-
çades it is affirmed
ds, elsewhere it is

ncord as the basis
common belief in
, where there was
etween the perfect
: human figure and
mony. Sir Henry
:nice, reflects some
writes :—

onances that most
:nt of all Nature, the
:of the first riseth
tween two and three,
.terval between one
| four, etc. Now if
rtions, from audible
 them as shall fall
bitably result from
ous Contentment to

 that architectural
cal harmonies, but
on were established
lly diffused. The
niverse was com-
nships of numbers,
within the triangle
e of the numbers
s and relationships
network of numbers
governed the works
orks of man should
l that a building
microcosm, of the
.arger scale in the
. Alberti's words
tently and with a
)erations," what is
so in architecture,
.he harmony of the
and religious, was
ad the satisfaction
:ic.

imilar convictions
s bring " des verités
: quitte pas son
d'être arrivé à la
xactness, precision,
overall controlling
 unchallengeable
:s, but a sort of
itly, while in the
used through the
ing, at Garches it
and the disposition

ich Palladio rested
:entury, when pro-
dividual sensibility
:r, in spite of the
ford him, occupies
The functionalist
mpt to re-assert a
:ective value of the
ude. Results can
:tion of a particular
arently accidental
itradition of this
mathematical pat-
: are the universal

ite of theory, both
andard, a mathe-
' natural beauty ";
a particular pro-
t the blocks should
: 5½ : 5. Corbusier
relationships by

parison with those of the villa by Le Corbusier
opposite. For all their differences of style and construction, in the mathematical basis of their design these
two buildings have an important factor in common.

modular grid

piano nobile

elevation

"natural beauty" that by Wren's definition is "from
geometry". Le Corbusier himself supplies the proportional numbering of the elevation and places the
ratio of the golden section beside his design.

modular grid

first floor plan

A : B = B : (A + B)

elevation

explanatory dimens
prising the suites o
gression from a 3 :
are numbered 12 :
The façade is div
units, the two cen
division by their c
The horizontal div
introduction of t
alongside the " nat
purely "customary
horizontal division:
figures show, the:
division into fifths-
approximately thre
surface to order an
Corbusier also div
but in his case h
units are partly un
the garden terrace
corresponding to
vertical divisions a
by the equation (8
zontally. In both
detail of dominan
upon subsidiary sy:
sion into arch and
parapet, that Pall
asperities of his cul
and pyramidal ele:
both to conceal a:
the volumes. Son
prerogatives of soli
of the " plan para
arched forms and
Corbusier at Garch
In the frame buil
wall structure, th
dominant, but the
roof. The quality
Corbusier has notic
structure, in the fr
the section. Perfo
vertical movement
sculptural quality
disappeared, and th
firm sectional tra:
volume. Extensio:
the established hor
replaced by free pla
section ; and the
equally severe ; as
had been turned
plexities of section
now transferred to
The shapefulness
Garches plan cont
interior which see
intellect only, open:
vacuum. There is
the organised and
the intellect it is c
plexing; and it see:
anywhere in it, at
palpable impression
can be absorbed fr
in the cruciform ha
a clue to the whole
and focused there.
equidistance betwe:
equal importance t
between. Allowed
treated as a singl
development of
arbitrary proceeding
tation, and accept
extension ; at Gar
consistently broken
is disintegrated, a:
dispersion of incid
ments of the centr:
of serial installation
ties of the plan.
The system of h

Colin Rowe, *The Mathematics of the Ideal Villa and Other Essays*
(comparative analysis of La Malcontenta by Palladio and Villa Stein in Garches by
Le Corbusier)

149

R 3 04

PARIS - 35 rue de Sèvres - VI°

le ler Octobre 1936

Mr A U S T I N

Wadsworth Athenœum

Box 1409

H A R T F O R D (Connecticut)

Cher Ami,

Après enquête faite auprès de l'expéditeur, il paraîtrait que
40 dessins de Louis SOUTER seulement ont été envoyés à votre adresse.
C'est donc par erreur que j'en annonçais cinquante.

Vous voici rassuré et moi aussi.

Je relis ma lettre du 5 Juin et votre lettre du 16 Juin pour me
rafraîchir les idées et je vois que vous êtes assez gentil pour organiser
une Exposition cet hiver à Hartford.

J'ai eu des nouvelles de Louis SOUTER qui s'ennuie beaucoup et qui
demande si quelques dessins ont pu se vendre. Vous voyez qu'en faisant une
œuvre gentille à l'égard d'un homme extrêmement intéressant, vous pourriez
acquérir pour bien peu de chose de magnifiques dessins. J'espère donc que
vous et vos amis du Musée pourrez acheter quelques dessins de SOUTER.

Dans votre lettre du 16 Juin, vous me dites très gentiment que mon
séjour a été trop court à Hartford. Je le trouve aussi, mais, hélas ! la
vie a ses exigences.

Je vais vous proposer une chose intéressante et voici laquelle :
je viens de passer deux mois à Rio de Janeiro où j'ai fait les plans du
Palais du Ministère de l'Education et, d'autre part, les plans de l'immense
Cité Universitaire qu'on projette de construire.

Je suis rentré sur un bateau italien et j'ai trouvé avec joie un
ancien ami, Alberto LANDSBERG qui est citoyen brésilien et qui allait passer
ses vacances dans sa villa "Malcontenta". En effet, LANDSBERG est l'heureux
propriétaire d'une des plus importantes créations de Palladio. Cette villa
qu'il a achetée à l'état de moulin et de hangard, il l'a nettoyée, mais
d'aplomb et découvert d'innombrables fresques de Véronèse. C'est d'ailleurs
un garçon qui a la passion des choses de l'art, il ne vit que pour cela.
C'était mon compagnon de table sur le bateau et nous avons eu des entretiens
agréables qui ont poursuivi ceux que j'avais déjà eux dans la villa elle-même.

Je revien

Le Corbusier, letter to Mr. Austin,
October 1, 1936

"[...] I traveled back on an Italian ship and
it was with great joy that I met an old friend,
Alberto LANDSBERG, a Brazilian, who
was going to spend his holidays at his villa
"Malcontenta." I might add that LANDS-
BERG is the lucky owner of one of
Palladio's most important works. Having
purchased the villa in a state of complete
dereliction, he has cleaned it up, restored

it and discovered countless frescoes by
Veronese. Moreover, he has a passion for
all things artistic, indeed it's his sole raison
d'etre. He was my dining companion
onboard and we had some very pleasant
discussions, along the same lines as those
we'd already had in the villa itself.
To return to what I was saying: one day
LANDSBERG said to me: How is it that
in the whole world, at present, there isn't a
single person or authority or any sort of
organization which has thought of taking

Je reviens à mon sujet : LANDSBERG m'a dit un jour ceci : Comment se fait-il qu'il n'y ait pas dans le monde entier, à l'heure actuelle, un homme ouune autorité ou une organisation quelconque qui ait l'idée de profiter de la présence à Paris d'un des groupes les plus extraordinaires que l'Art ait engendrés à la même époque et qu'il ne profite pas de faire construire une villa ou un édifice modeste avec cette collaboration éblouissante que l'histoire n'a pour ainsi dire jamais connue. Il parlait de la présence à Paris de gens comme Fernand LEGER, comme PICASSO, comme BRAQUE, comme Henri LAURENS, Jacques LIPCHITZ, BRANCUSSI, etc... et il me disait que tous ces hommes étant mes amis, de même âge à peu près, et l'architecture étant actuellement en train de prendre une forme nouvelle, l'occasion serait unique de grouper tout ce monde et de faire une chose qui compterait désormais.

J'avoue que l'idée me paraît en effet juste et ce qui m'a intéressé c'est qu'en effet tous les noms cités ci-dessus représentent des individus qui sont tous préparés les Temps Nouveaux des arts liés à l'architecture ; aucun n'a jamais participé à une oeuvre commune de pureté esthétique. Les milliards s'en vont à toutes sortes de sottises. Je me charge de pouvoir mettre tous ces camarades en collaboration dans une chose à grande portée architecturale. Qui peut être le manager de cette affaire ? La France déchirée dans ses passions politiques est loin d'y penser et quand elle y pense, elle y pense bougrement mal (Exposition de 1937).

L'Amérique est en plein renouveau, en pleine curiosité. Vous et le Museum of Modern Art avez organisé les plus solennelles manifestations de l'art moderne dans le monde. Ne croyez-vous pas que, sous l'égide du Musée d'Hartford, un industriel quelconque serait heureux de devenir détenteur d'une oeuvre assurée d'une valeur financière indiscutable et d'une signification morale la plus haute. J'ajoute que je suis persuadé de pouvoir, en groupant mes amis peintres et sculpteurs, leur faire quitter leurs fameuses cotes de bourse qui sont tout à fait prohibitives et leur faire admettre pour des sommes raisonnables une pleine collaboration.

N'est-ce pas un joli sujet à envisager, puisque nous nous connaissons bien et que je vous promets mon concours, n'est-ce pas une assez coquette entreprise à méditer au coin du feu avec nos amis SOBY et HITCHCOCK ? Dans cinq ans ce sera trop tard et dans dix ans.... nous serons tous morts.

Amicalement à vous et amitiés aux amis.

---

advantage of the presence in Paris of one of the most extraordinary groups produced by Art at the same time, or of building a villa or a modest building using the most dazzling collaboration ever known to history? He was referring to the presence in Paris of men like Fernand LEGER, like PICASSO, like BRAQUE, like Henri LAURENS, Jacques LIPCHITZ, BRANCUSI, etc.... Moreover, he said that since all those men are my friends, and about the same age as me, and given that architecture was in the process of assuming a new form, it would be a unique opportunity to bring all these people together and make something that would matter from now on. [...]"

of his rooms, and the philosophical concepts underlying his formation. Wittkower would return to these same topics many years later, at the height of his career, and the resulting chapters are now regarded as benchmarks in Palladian historiography.[84]

Therefore life seemed to continue in the house along the lines that had been laid down over the years. **Kenneth Clark** arrived in May 1935, just after he had been appointed as Director of the National Gallery in London and Surveyor of the King's Pictures. In September Philip Alexius de László, at the height of his success as a portrait painter, visited;[85] then Serge Lifar returned the following day. Arturo-José Lopez-Willshaw arrived in September the following year, this time in the company of his wife Patricia (who, a few years later, would declare unhesitatingly that she had never set foot in Rue du Centre before she married). Marion Phillimore returned in June, together with Claud. In short, the same names appear, time and time again, coupled with those of Princess Vittoria Eugenia of Savoia, Marina of Russia, Princess Galitzin, and Virginia Agnelli who was accompanied on this occasion by Princess Marina Colonna.

––––––

After visiting the house, the guest was almost always invited— in a gesture that almost took the form of a ritual—to walk in the garden, which, over the course of ten seasons or so, was now quite mature.

The geometric designs were clearly visible: from the path that circled in front of the building and then penetrated a series of flower-filled secret gardens at the sides of the villa, to the paths that formed a grid to the south of the house—parallel to the old carriageway—as if to mark the outline of an ideal forum in classical times.

Here, too, on the outside—mirroring the interior—the setting was punctuated by references, which served in turn to test the visitor's cultural knowledge or as a prompt for conversation. Those benches lining the approach to the inlet (positioned as if the master of the house might wait there for a visitor arriving by gondola from Venice) echoed the design of the benches depicted by Pozzoserrato in a famous painting; that circular island was known as "rabbit island" because the rabbits—

instinctively averse to water—would not leave their moated enclosure; the "secret gardens" were an abstract interpretation of the courtyards that Palladio had intended to create at the sides of the house.

The small residence, which Le Corbusier had suggested might serve as the *buen ritiro* for the owner of a modern building, whose architecture could be just as peremptory as Palladio's own, can be discovered by walking down the so-called west avenue.

To the south of this avenue stands a small building, a glasshouse, which was evidence of Paul's ability to design a construction in which modernity was seamlessly merged with traditional forms.

The far end of this open land south of the house, at the furthest extremity of the avenues, is a celebration of Paul's art as advisor. Unless prompted by Catherine to admire the peach orchard, planted at her instigation in the fields to the west of the garden, on the other side of a low wall, it was here that the guests' attention was drawn by Bertie's gentle voice back to the Palladian architecture; they would turn to look at the south façade, which—even when seen from a distance—appears enigmatic, eluding all attempts, however cultured, to decipher its secrets.

If Bertie realized that the guests were not following his erudite explanations about the design of the *bugnato* (ashlar work), or about the Ionic order of the front façade, whose entablature was broken, one might say, by the unexpected inclusion of a thermal window, he would then start to talk— with a slight smile—about the large circular chimneys, topped by two small domes, almost like minarets. In the same way, on his way back to the house, he would hesitate a moment, almost as if to encourage one of his guests to ask about the provenance and significance of the large balls of trachyte, which lined the edge of the lawn not far from the façade.

In the course of such conversation, without being pressed for time, it would begin to grow dark. At dusk, a guest might pick a spray of orange blossom or flowering jasmine. If they were invited to stay for dinner, the menu would very probably include a "Brazilian soup" (made from carrots and milk), followed by a dish of hard-boiled eggs served with radicchio.

In the meantime, the ceremony of lighting dozens of strate-gically positioned candles would occur, as it did every evening. Guests were aware that their perception sharpened as their pupils slowly dilated, and as the mind—governed by its mysteri-ous workings—elaborated the frescoed images and restored a perfect view of them, one that seemed to deny the existence of those damaged areas that were mercilessly revealed by sunlight.

When all were finally seated at table, and if the guests staying at La Malcontenta were of particular interest, a game was played, not unlike the one that involves trying to guess the date, authenticity, and provenance of a particular item.

For example, if George Matei Cantacuzino was present, it did not matter that he was a liberal intellectual educated at the École des Beaux-Arts (the School of Fine Arts); instead what really interested those present was to discover the Byzantine dynasty to which his family belonged, and to guess when his forebears had occupied the imperial throne in Constantinople. Or if **Lydia di Sangro** arrived, the debate—however fruitless—would again focus on whether the di Sangro family descended from Charlemagne, from the celebrated Berengario, Italy's first king, or from Oderisio the Longobard. Likewise, one not only had to know that **Princess of Polignac**'s palace in Venice dated from the early Renaissance, but also that her father, **Isaac Singer**, had left her a fortune made by invading the world with his own brand of sewing machines. Or in the case of Norah Lindsay, the game consisted of guess-ing the name of the wealthy client who had commissioned the large garden she was about to finish.

This way of fragmenting the past—both the remote past and more recent times—is a process that seems intentionally designed to forestall any overall vision, one that could be interpreted as history. It is a deliberate choice to let time pass without acknowledging the centuries and the years, let alone the hours and the minutes: a choice that blends well with the decision not to be subordinate to any necessity.

This mental attitude is the same that led, as we have already seen, to an exaltation of objects for their unique quality, for the unrepeatable specificity of their beauty, and for the silence surrounding them: a silence that alone can withstand the noise of meaning and cataloguing. In short, Bertie continued to live as if he were set apart from fate, and as if he could escape every impelling action, even death itself, which is our common destiny (the ultimate destination, to use the words of Sophocles which Paul had tried to teach Bertie without success).

Paul defined this attitude as *frivolitas divina*. While Paul was absorbed in his aristocratic isolation, he did seem to have a clearer perception than Bertie of the tragedy that was unfolding in Europe. Instead the latter, in order to safeguard his vision of the world, had segmented reality into sealed compartments, and had excluded work and politics from the circle of interests to which he dedicated his attention.[86]

It may have been the news that Aby Warburg's vast library had been hurriedly moved from Hamburg to London that made Bertie aware—for the first time—of the nature of the Nazi regime. But even this knowledge did not prompt a train of thought that might have led to a decision. However, in his subconscious, he was close to a crisis point. Nothing except for a crisis would have convinced him to allow an unquantifiable number of strangers enter his house, whose doors had, until then, only been opened to carefully chosen guests.

He decided to accept an offer to publish images of the villa, its rooms, and its decorations in a magazine with a large circulation. But, unlike Paul who had not written a single word commenting on the photos of the house in Neuilly when it had been published in *Art et industrie*, Bertie could not refrain from acting as guide to the virtual visitor who would visit his house on paper and even discover its interior beauty.

However, Bertie may not have realized that the mere act of taking a pen in hand would undermine that untrammeled passing of time by which he had, until then, been lulled. Preparing himself to talk about the villa as something other than himself—and having to do so without being able to talk face to face with his interlocutor, and without being able to use the charm of his elegant manners, the suggestion of his observations, and the evocative power of his memories raised the disturbing awareness that the way of life he had lived up until this moment might have reached a turning point.

An operation of this kind could not be commenced, therefore, without profound inner agitation.

When completing this writing task Bertie's psychological anguish was so intense that it resulted in an effort that was almost overwhelming. An endless stream of corrections, changes, and erasures covered the sheets on which he tried to sum up his experience, in an attempt to give a coherent form or order to the tumult of memories and thoughts that were jumbled in his mind.

His account starts on an almost hesitant note. An English traveler, he wrote, who did not know that this building had been constructed in the mid-sixteenth century, would not be at all surprised to see a prominent portico on its façade, accustomed as he was to the buildings designed in his native land by Inigo Jones, Wren, Kent, and later the Adam brothers.

However, as Bertie progressed, a feeling of pride emerges from his writing. He asserts his own part in having discovered one of the greatest testimonials of European architecture in a state of complete dereliction; he is at pains to show how he understood its secrets better than anyone else, and he claims recognition for the purity of the cultural approach he used and through which he revitalized the building without violating its essence. It is as if he was writing solely for the benefit of the specialists who visited the *palazzo*, even in these last months, in order to study its proportions and admire its harmony.[87]

When introducing the virtual public inside the walls of the *palazzo*, however, Bertie made a significant omission. He did not mention the love affairs and the many tensions— whether intellectual or mischievous—that the rooms of the villa had witnessed for over ten years. In the pages he wrote, these spaces are not brought to life by anyone, whether guest or friend. It is as if Bertie had had the presentiment that the rooms of his house were destined, all of a sudden, to remain empty.

In the silence that was left, as these echoes gradually died out, Bertie became increasingly aware that he had been the protagonist of an unrepeatable adventure: an adventure that was both emotional and intellectual, during which he had singled out for himself an autonomous and original field of action. Namely, he had conceived, devised, and implemented a theory of building conservation that no one had ever before

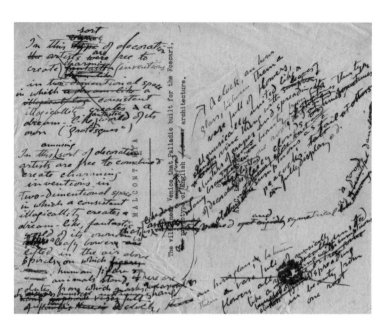

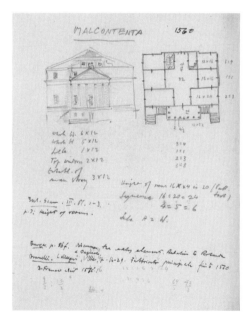

Bertie Landsberg, "An Historic Italian Villa, Malcontenta," draft (t.);
and published in *Country Life*, October 16, 1937 (b.l.)
Rudolf Wittkower, "Malcontenta, Study of the proportional criteria used
in the architecture," 1930s (b.r.)

Catherine d'Erlanger, *"Baba," d'Erlanger*, 1931;
Serge Lifar

Catherine d'Erlanger, female figure; male figure

practiced with such rigor. Moreover, this had helped to divulge knowledge of the important heritage represented by the villas dotted about the Veneto countryside. It was as if Bertie, for the first time, realized the full extent of the cultural role he had played and how he could claim merit for it without creating emotional agitation.

A process of this kind, at the same time a liberation and a renunciation, was clearly determined by what was now the irreversible crisis affecting the trio—namely Paul, Catherine, and himself—that had served as the foundation for his psychological equilibrium. Paul's absence was a crucial factor, and Catherine's was no less important, because the Baroness, as well as having been the mainstay in a complex psychological relationship, had been the person who brought a vital force to La Malcontenta as well as an organizational ability that neither Bertie nor Paul possessed.

That Catherine had undergone a profound change can be seen, even superficially, in the paintings that she produced. No longer were these portraits carried out using traditional techniques, or using realistic features, in pastel colors. Now instead she used the most variegated materials: fabric, lace, and buttons, all mixed up in thick layers of color. Her painting had become visibly more resolute, more experimental, almost provocative, revealing the new impulses that had matured in her character.

Not only had she decided to leave behind the *palazzo*, which she had once likened to Palladio "singing songs in stone,"[88] she was now ready to leave Italy, and Europe, and even the d'Erlanger family. She would not wait for Mussolini's government to approve the Manifesto of Race, aligning Italian legislation with Nazi theorizing on racial purity nor for a decree regulating the presence of foreign Jews in Italy. All the prompting that she needed was the example of those intellectuals who had already left Europe. Or, perhaps even more simply, she acted on instinct.

Her departure instantly reversed that centripetal attraction which had kept the balance—like the planets being maintained in equilibrium through gravity—between lives that were founded on different existential premises.

Bertie had always been convinced that no principle of causality could determine the outcome of a story, whether positive or negative, and therefore, in the absence of a true story, there could be no real *novitas*.

Catherine—that intuitive woman who, to use Paul Morand's words, knew everything without even having opened a book—was, by nature, permanently waiting for *novitas*. She was always ready to seize the subversive essence in every manifestation of the spirit. She was always in search of her own destiny.

Bertie had put down roots at La Malcontenta, like the willows he had planted along the Riviera. He believed, or rather he wanted to believe, that the visits by **Margherita Sarfatti, Princess Vittoria Eugenia di Savoia,** and **Virginia Agnelli**— whom he regarded as emblems of the Fascist regime, of Italy's monarchy, and of its capitalist enterprises—would alone be sufficient to confirm that Mussolini's government would maintain a neutral position towards the Jewish community, as had been the case until then. Because it suited his way of thinking, he supported the interpretation of events that even a figure of unquestionable integrity, such as the Chief Rabbi of Rome, expressed in the messages he sent out to his fellow believers in Venice, with whom Bertie was in contact.[89]

Catherine did not entertain any such illusions. She left. She traveled without a second thought to another country: the United States. Once there, she headed for California (as Thomas Mann had once done, to name just one of the many who might have influenced her choice). She settled in Holly-wood, at the heart of the film industry that was glaring beacon of the Europe set to disapear, and the beginning of a new cultural trend.

She did not arrive there alone. Catherine was not the type to appear in public without a companion. Once again she was flanked by a good-looking man, an artist whose muse she aspired to be. His name was **John Walsh**, and he was a young Australian singer. Catherine bought a large house at Number 8795, Sunset Boulevard, and before long—after her husband's death—she had opened a club there, known as *The Café Gala*, with a dramatic view of the city. "The decor was red and white. Striped wallpaper, red matchbooks with an imprint of a Venetian mark, and white-gloved waiters." The club was instantly successful and within a matter of weeks became an iconic venue of Hollywood life. The elitist circle of homosexuals in the film industry gathered here; Cole Porter would come to play the piano, and later **Judy Garland** and **Frank Sinatra** would also sing here.

Catherine's departure—even before this further emancipation from the rules, which she had tried to respect, for form at least—was also a sort of challenge, a gauntlet that she threw down for Bertie, knowing that he would not pick it up. This is borne out by the fact that she left him much of the furniture from the *Casa Rosa*, which she owned on the Riva degli Schiavoni.

———

This gift helped Bertie to turn his mind to the house's furnishings and decor, which had reached a rare level of perfection, maintained as they were in that sophisticated state of semi-abandonment. It was an odd collection of ornaments and furniture which Giuseppe Volpi had noted, with some perplexity, a few years earlier would only be appropriate in a space occupied with *sprezzatura* (nonchalance), by a "sincerely eccentric family": to the extent that it "was in part Plato's Banquet and in part the Abbey of Thelema," to repeat the phrase used by Paul Morand in 1927.[90]

When this dimension was absent, the set-up was in a sense not genuine: therefore, it could no longer be justified, even at a social level. This state of affairs became even more pressing when Volpi—the key figure in the cosmopolitan world of the Film Festival—started to restore a famous Palladian building, which he had bought earlier (in 1934); therefore, in the eyes of the "fashionable world," it was Volpi who began to be seen as the savior of the great architect's Renaissance legacy.

Bertie was well aware of all this because **Marina Volpi**, who helped her father in this adventure, often arrived on the banks of the Brenta to consult Bertie and to arrange yet another visit to Maser, the site of the villa that had belonged to **Daniele Barbaro**, Patriarch of Aquileia, and his brother **Marcantonio,** who was one of the powerful Procurators of San Marco, Palladio's grand patrons. Bertie never failed to help Marina, even if he felt that haste and money could all too easily undermine the sense of respect and love that a work of art

Catherine d'Erlanger's house in Hollywood, interior, 1946
Catherine d'Erlanger beside the pool at her house in Hollywood, 1946

deserved.[91] Instead he kept repeating to Marina that it was better to hang a faded tapestry over a lacuna in the plaster rather than renew the entire wall; and that a Mameluke carpet— if one was lucky enough to find one—cost less than the proper repair work to an antique terrazzo floor.

On his way to Maser, Bertie came across a small town, which he would almost certainly have found attractive; Asolo is indeed a very charming spot, standing on a hill from which, on particularly clear days, one can see Venice.

As we might have imagined, now that we know him a little better, Bertie was fascinated by the idea that a royal court had resided here in the early sixteenth century, centered around the figure of **Caterina Cornaro**, the Venetian noblewoman who handed the Kingdom of Cyprus, which she had inherited from her husband, over to Venice. Bertie was equally attracted by the figure of **Pietro Bembo**, who had been a member of that court and its leading intellectual, because Bembo had pursued an ambitious ideal, which a generation later inspired the great literary scholar, **Giangiorgio Trissino**, who was Andrea Palladio's first patron.

Both Pietro Bembo and Giangiorgio Trissino were convinced that a unification of the mosaic of political units that made up Italy at the time could be achieved—at least ideally— through a process of linguistic unification. It was for this purpose that Pietro Bembo had decided to codify the Italian language by founding it on Petrarch's literary legacy. For his part, Giangiorgio Trissino had educated Palladio to develop an architectural language based on the canons of Vitruvius.

It was to ponder and elaborate on these thoughts that Bertie frequently returned to the hill of Asolo, escorted by handsome young chauffeurs, whom he chose in the same way that, in Venice, he took care to select personally the gondoliers who would transport him.[92]

———

Here in Asolo, as well as being captivated by the charm of the town and the beauty of the countryside over which it looked— Bertie was fascinated by the old-fashioned methods with which, in a seventeenth-century building (one that the English artist **Herbert Young Hammerton** had used as a studio earlier in the century), yarn was twisted and boiled, and then skeins dyed before being woven on antique looms. This activity had been started in 1840 by a lively American journalist; it had then been taken over by **Flora Stark**, an English woman of considerable initiative with whom Bertie enjoyed many long conversations.

It was during these meetings—which increasingly took the form of a monologue, as Bertie became more and more excited as he perfected his idea—that he suggested Flora Stark should follow the example set twenty years earlier by **Mariano Fortuny**. In a vast, almost decrepit Venetian *palazzo*, which Bertie had visited years earlier, as soon as he arrived in Venice, this uniquely talented Spaniard had started to produce textiles that conjured up the elegance of the Orient, with Byzantine influences. Palazzo Pesaro was not the atelier in Rue de la Rouche, where Paul now went, but it exerted a not dissimilar fascination: specialized craftsmen dyed cloths using egg-white primers, and fashioned garments with countless pleats, in the same way as the artisans who worked for Jean-Michel Frank used to apply parchment or shagreen to minimalist furniture.

An idea was taking shape in Bertie's mind: the weaving shop in Asolo could attain the same level of quality and produce fabrics replicating—in terms of weight, material, design, and colors—those depicted in the paintings and frescos by sixteenth century Venetian artists, and above all by Veronese.

Bertie was prompted to suggest the idea because Marina Volpi had been pressing him for indications on how to proceed with the furnishing of the Palladian villa at Maser, which her father had almost finished restoring. Moreover, Catherine's furniture from the *Casa Rosa*, which she had left to him before leaving, had now been delivered to La Malcontenta. Therefore when Bertie held in his hands the first fabrics, still smelling of dye, produced by Flora Stark's looms, he decided—in a moment of happiness that he had not dreamed of finding again—to renew the interior décor of the villa. This was a delicate operation, because the fabrics were light and perishable, but it would also prove highly effective because the new materials and the new colors lent the house a sense of freshness; at the same time he would be able to establish an ideal link between the present and the past by carefully matching the colors of the fabrics with those of the frescos.

Bertie did not possess the skills to manage an operation of this kind efficiently. He engaged an assistant whose job was to oversee the orders, deliveries, and payments: tasks that were undertaken first by **Sybil Lubbock**, and then by **Lilly Mueller**. In October, in order to ensure that the whole project would be completed on time, Bertie postponed his departure and moved into the Hotel Danieli in Venice.

His visits to Asolo also gave him the opportunity to get to know Freya, Flora Stark's daughter: she was adventurous and enterprising, with an intelligence that was at once both lucid and ironic. She and Catherine had completely different interests—indeed, Freya's interests recalled those of Robert Byron and they evoked the fascination of the Orient, which acted on Bertie's subconscious like a dose of nostalgia.

These were the weeks between 1937 and 1938. **Freya Stark** had already been to Mesopotamia and Egypt, as well as in Transjordania and Palestine, and on her return from Western Iran she was awarded the prestigious Back Memorial Prize by the Royal Geographical Society for the discoveries that crowned her archaeological career. In 1934 she had achieved great success with the publication of her book, *The Valley of Assassins*; now she was writing another one, an account of her journey in the Hadhramaut, which would soon earn her the Founder's Gold Medal from the Royal Geographical Society.

In Freya Stark Bertie found almost everything to satisfy his curiosity; above all she opened up horizons free from any social implications. Moreover, she possessed precisely the political culture Catherine lacked, even if only in the quasi-Victorian sense of the term. Like many English intellectuals of her generation, she had also undertaken intelligence work for the British crown. Her extensive travels throughout the territories of the former Ottoman Empire, which had become a British protectorate after the First World War, had provided her with a virtually unrivalled knowledge of the Mesopotamian area (where most of the British oil interests were concentrated). This enabled her to express precise (and sadly prophetic) opinions on the outcomes of the Arab-Israeli tensions, which had already started to appear in Palestinian territory.

Telefono: Mira 37.

Villa della Malcontenta,
Malcontenta,
Venezia.

17ᵗʰ Nov. 1937

My dear Miss Stark,

Thank you for sending me the enclosed sample. It is splendid. Just the good, strong weave that is required. Also your idea of mixing the two colours is excellent. The black dividing threads I do not like (as you will see I have pulled them out!) If you agree with me a light pinkish brown thread (dividing one side only of the two colours) might be added? The

Bertie Landsberg, letter to Flora Stark,
November 17, 1937

"[…] Thank you for sending me the enclosed
sample. It is splendid. Just the good,
strong weave that is required. Also your
idea of mixing the two colours is excellent.
The black dividing threads I do not like
(as you will see I have pulled them out!).
If you agree with me a light pinkish brown
thread (dividing one side only of the two
colours) might be added? The green might
possibly be a little lighter, in any case
it should not be darker. The pinkish colour
is perfect, and your idea of mixing a little
green in it is an inspiration. […]"

167

The Friends of Malcontenta, "Aide-toi, le ciel t'aidera"; "On n'est jamais mieux servi que par soi-même" (gentle reminders written to invite the Friends of Malcontenta to help themselves during their stay); *Summer Residential Club*, 1939, front cover and p. 5

THESE NAMES MAKE NEWS

No Malcontents There

A N old house comes to life. . . .
First Lord of the Admiralty's Lady DIANA COOPER, rich, USA-born Lady RIBBLESDALE, National Gallery's Sir KENNETH CLARKE, middlebrow literature's Sir HUGH WALPOLE are on informal committee which is to help run La Malcontenta, famous villa near Venice, as residential country club.

This club might really be what every club would like to dare to be—"exclusive"; for there's only room for about a dozen people to stay there, and names of committee indicate that members will mostly belong to the tidier intelligentsia.

VILLA belongs to connoisseur A. C. ("Bertie") LANDSBERG, who will still stay on as host; profits from 10-guinea entrance-fees, £1-a-day rates (Italian drinks included) will be used for uncovering & restoring villa's 16th-century frescoes.

Until Landsberg bought it it had stood empty for a century & a half, the last of the Foscari family for whom it was built having squandered his wealth as Venetian Ambassador in St Petersburg.

"Perhaps," writes OSBERT SITWELL, "as it stared with a bleak & classical gaze over this flat land, it had seemed almost too severe to live in . . ." It was "given over . . . to the storing of grain, the drying of grapes upon mats laid on the floor in the golden sunshine that streamed in at the unglazed windows, and to the white fluttering of doves as they cooed & circled under the arched recesses & dome of the banqueting high central hall."

INNER walls were whitewashed. Landsberg found old guidebooks describing frescoes by Veronese, Zelotti, other artists.
He would choose a blank wall at random, climb a ladder with guidebook in one hand, sponge in other, dab tentatively with sponge; mistily from the whitewash

La Malcontenta

"A bleak & classical gaze"

emerged "the rose-pink foot of Daphne fleeing across flowered lawns."

MALCONTENTA was built in 1555 by architect Palladio, after whom is called the Palladian style which in England you can see at Chiswick House or Stowe School or Mereworth Castle (pronounced Merryworth), Kent home of the Hon Esmond Harmsworth. Mereworth is copied from villa.

WHAT'S ON

This Morning

100 YEARS OF T.P.O.
Centenary of the Travelling Post Office is being celebrated at Euston from 10.30, when Postmaster-General Tryon, Lord Mayor of London Sir Harry Twyford, and L.M.S Chairman Sir Josiah Stamp are foregathering at the station. Later in the morning you will be able to see exhibition of T.P.O.'s advance in 100 years from horse-box temporarily fitted up as a sorting carriage to present-day grandeur of green-baize-topped tables, H. and C.

SINGLES
Paddington Club Tennis Tournament starts at 10 with ladies' singles. Today's players include Shella Paterson, Valerie Scott, Gladys Mathias. 1/6 to watch. Station, Maida Vale, 2 minutes' walk.

WELL SPENT MONEY?
Intricate laundering machinery on view at the International Hall, Islington, in the International Laundry Exhibition. Thousands are spent every year in an effort to keep buttons on your shirts; and all else in order at the laundry. Official opening 12.45. Open to public afterwards.

This Afternoon

SPRING FALL
Fall of lambs (farmers' way of saying lambs born) is more than average this year. 1½ lambs per ewe (usually there are 1.2 or 1.3 lambs per ewe). Good fields-full to see at Alresford in Hampshire, Aylesbury (Bucks), Maldon (Essex), Sawbridgeworth (Herts), Chessington (Surrey).

built by Palladio for his own retirement near Vicenza, his home-town.

*

I SPENT a night this week-end only a few miles from Mereworth—at the green, fertile, beer-brewing village of Wateringbury.
Great excitement in the village; biggest crowd the church room had ever held; inaugural meeting of ARP. . . .
At the door, the entire local police force (one sergeant, one constable). On the platform, meeting's conveners (an admiral, an insurance broker).
Some brisk discussion, a few red herrings; then the admiral appealed for volunteers over 30.
Shyness, hanging-back; so he said was there anybody over 30 who would not volunteer.
Altogether twenty-eight gave in their names: baker, bricklayer, retired colonial governor, farm bailiff, metal broker—representative selection from the 150 or so who were there (village's whole population is about 1,000).

*

ON cross-country—weather was better than I'd feared—to near Heathfield (which the locals, in my young days, used to pronounce Heffull, but I suppose the BBC has taught them better now).
I wanted to call at another old house which has come to life—house as different from the villa Malcontenta as the Sussex landscape is from the Italian: warm red brick, log fires, a tench-pool, a barn.
Novelist JOHN HEYGATE bought it only a year or two ago; did it up elaborately; wrote a book about it, which suggested that he, his lovely ex-film-star wife, their newly-born child were settled there for life.
He is already selling; London was too strong for them.

IT seems a pity. Local paper commented acidly on writers from London who buy country homes, make books out of them, then leave.
"But," said Mrs Heygate, "if only they'd buy a lot more of the books we wouldn't have to leave."

THAT book—"A House for Joanna"—was by no means unsuccessful; but to run a country home as well as a London flat is certainly too much for most of us.
Having lived in London for ten

years, I now want to live in the country; so acquired, amid chaos of Heygates' removal, some bits of furniture they didn't need.
When I have found the house I want I shall take it; but I hope I shall be able to resist the temptation to exploit for this column what fragments of privacy are left me.

*

DESPITE note in this column on Wednesday, naturalisation applicants are still being sold copies of rules containing oath of allegiance to Edward VIII.
No change, say Stationery Office, till present printing is sold out.
How many were printed Only 250, but they don't sell very well; people prefer form itself, not a copy.

COLLEAGUE who called at Stationery Office noticed several things:—
Man at special inquiry counter has notice up by him saying that if a man can preach a better sermon, write a better book or make a better mousetrap than his neighbour, the world will beat a path to his door.
Dressy young man was worrying about traffic-sign regulations. "They all seem to be amendments of each other," he said. "Will it cost the earth to buy them?"
It cost 9d.
A voice in the background was intoning "And YOU are the Borough Surveyor of Ilkeston, Derbyshire?"

*

SOUTHERN RAILWAY earn bouquet for bringing you this column.
Writing in the "depths" of the country, I wanted to send it up by train. No reply from nearest station when I tried to ring it.
"They are not in attendance on Sunday," said exchange, formally, "unless there's a train about."
So I rang Victoria inquiries, asked when there was a train; said I wanted to send letter up, didn't say I was Press.
Of their own accord they arranged for local station to put MS on train for Brighton; for Brighton to transfer it to London train.
I only hope it got there.

William Hickey

William Hickey, "No Malcontents There," *Daily Express*, March 28, 1938

It was these meetings with this resolute woman, who was
so honest in her expressions and so well informed, that allowed
Bertie gradually to come to terms with, and finally overcome,
the psychological doubts that until then had prevented him
from acknowledging the gravity of the European political situation. He finally understood he would have to leave a house
he had come to identify with and whose continued existence
throughout the centuries represented an unchanging fate he
might have wished for himself.

The decision to bring into the house the freshness of
those newly dyed fabrics, which also revived the fading colors
of the frescos, was not a mere whim. Instead, it was an act
of extreme love, the kind gesture that preceded a detachment.
It was almost an antidote, albeit an abstract one, that helped
to free Bertie from the frantic rhythm of visitors arriving at the
villa during the summer months of 1938.

As if taking part in a ritual farewell to a world destined
to change, the house witnessed the appearance—together
with the **Princess of Russia**, the **Queen Mother of Greece**,
and **Princess Eugenia**—of that Princess Bibesco whom we
previously encountered at Catherine's house in Paris, and
of Caio de Mello Franco and his sister Luci, Arturo-José, and
Volpi's daughter, alternated with visits by countless others
coming in and out of the villa's doors like a curtain call.

Berie painfully prepared his exit. As the manager—which
he still hoped to be in this setting—he was concerned not
to leave the stage empty. On account of the love he felt for this
building, he was worried about the serious risks posed to its
conservation if it became known that it was empty.

Already with one foot over the threshold, enveloped
by the scent of jasmine, he virtually handed the house keys to
an informal association of people who, starting from May 1
the following year, that fateful 1939, would be able to use the
palazzo as a Summer Residential Club.

"The Palace can accommodate up to 14 persons,"
stated the regulations drawn up by a committee of eminent
society figures, including Diana Cooper, who'd been a
habitual visitor to the house for years, and Norah Lindsay
who regularly stayed here whenever she came to Venice.[93]

"The famous villa built by Palladio" was presented as
the highlight of every visit to Venice and the Lido, and of every
excursion across the vast plain stretching from Urbino to
Mantua and north to Udine.

The political reality of the day barely figures, if not for the
latent concern that the *Friends of Malcontenta* be mistaken
for some sort of anti-fascist association. Therefore, in order to
reassure the local party officials, the brochure went on to
state that the association was an "entirely informal agreement
between friends."

However, the publicity given to the initiative in an important
English newspaper by **Sir Hugh Walpole**, the celebrated
novelist, proved useless. The "club" would not even have the
time to meet once on the banks of the Brenta. The racist
legislation introduced by the Italian government in October
dramatically sealed the alliance between Fascism and Nazism.

––––––

A young journalist visited La Malcontenta, perhaps by chance,
just a few days after these worrying political developments.
One section in the final article she wrote was called "The invisi-
ble guest."[94] She felt the absence of the individuals who, for
the past fifteen years, had brought this architecture to life. The
only signs of Bertie's presence in the silent house were the
antique editions of Andrea Palladio's treatise on architecture—
carefully exhibited, and laid open at the pages illustrating
the *fabbrica* constructed for the "magnificent Signori Nicolò
and Alvise de' Foscari"—and engravings depicting the enigmatic face of the young king of France who had visited the house
in 1574.

In the article she described how an elegant young
man walked alone on the lawn in front of the south façade,
with a cockatoo perched on his arm (a reference to Paolo
Veronese? a tribute to Giambattista Tiepolo? an act of homage
to the spirit of Byron?). In the meantime, continued the
journalist, dense clouds passed so low over the *palazzo* that
they almost snagged on the chimneys, which rose high above
the roof.

These clouds, soon to unleash a tempest, signaled the end
of a season that had commenced with the shock of Giacomo
Matteotti's kidnapping and assassination.

Until the last, Bertie tried desperately to stay on the banks of the Brenta. But when Great Britain—"his real fatherland," as Claud always pointed out—declared war against Nazi Germany, he could not go on deluding himself. He finally made up his mind to leave, as the visitors' book in the villa records: "On Sept. 26th 1939 A.C.L. sailed for Rio de Janeiro, Brazil."

That Bertie would sooner or later have been forced to take a decision of this kind had been clearly understood, for some time, by a rich American lady from Connecticut. **Dorothea Mauran Watts** (whose considerable shareholdings in the oil company Shell allowed her to travel the world in style) did not need to follow European political events to understand that everything was changing. All she needed to know was that Catherine—the female element balancing the trio that had seemed unassailable in its solidity—had departed, and therefore the way was clear for her to visit La Malcontenta in June 1938, and to return in March 1939. It was then that Dorothea said to Bertie, "You are fifty, I'm fifty. Our ages total one hundred."[95]

Dorothea returned to the *palazzo* the day before Bertie's departure for Brazil on September 26, 1939. He went to his family home in Petropolis and, before long, Dorothea joined him. On March 20, 1940 they married and settled in Newport, Rhode Island. They only returned to "war-battered and dilapidated" La Malcontenta in April 1947.

On April 23 that year, after a frugal celebration with **Antonio Teodato** and his wife **Pasqua (Adele) Casotto**, who had confidently awaited the return of the owner whose lands they continued to farm, Bertie took out the visitors' book, which he had been given by Catherine more than twenty years before, and—together with Dorothea—started to collect the signatures of anyone who came to visit. It was as if nothing had happened between 1939 and 1947.

During the Eight years
of the war, the whole
N.W. column was covered
by ivy (Photograph 1947)

Dorothea and I

Bertie and Dorothea Landsberg after returning to La Malcontenta from
the United States, 1947

173

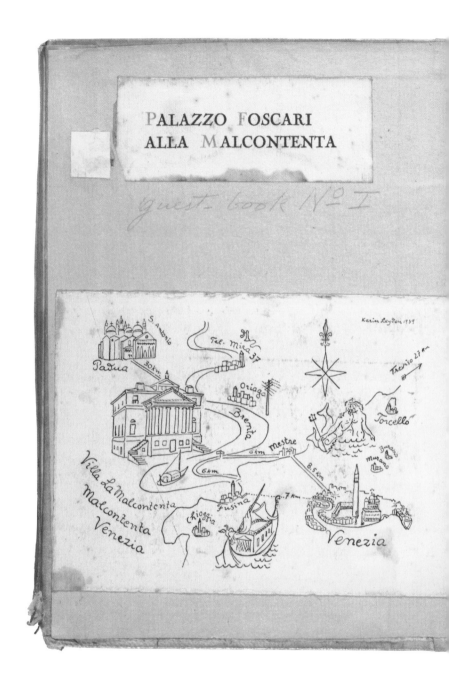

Visitors' book of La Malcontenta, pp. 1, 2

Bertie Landsberg

Signatures in the visitors' book: Norah Lindsay, Misia Sert, Diana Cooper, and others, August 1926, p. 10; Cole Porter, Howard Sturges, and others, October 2, 1926, p. 15

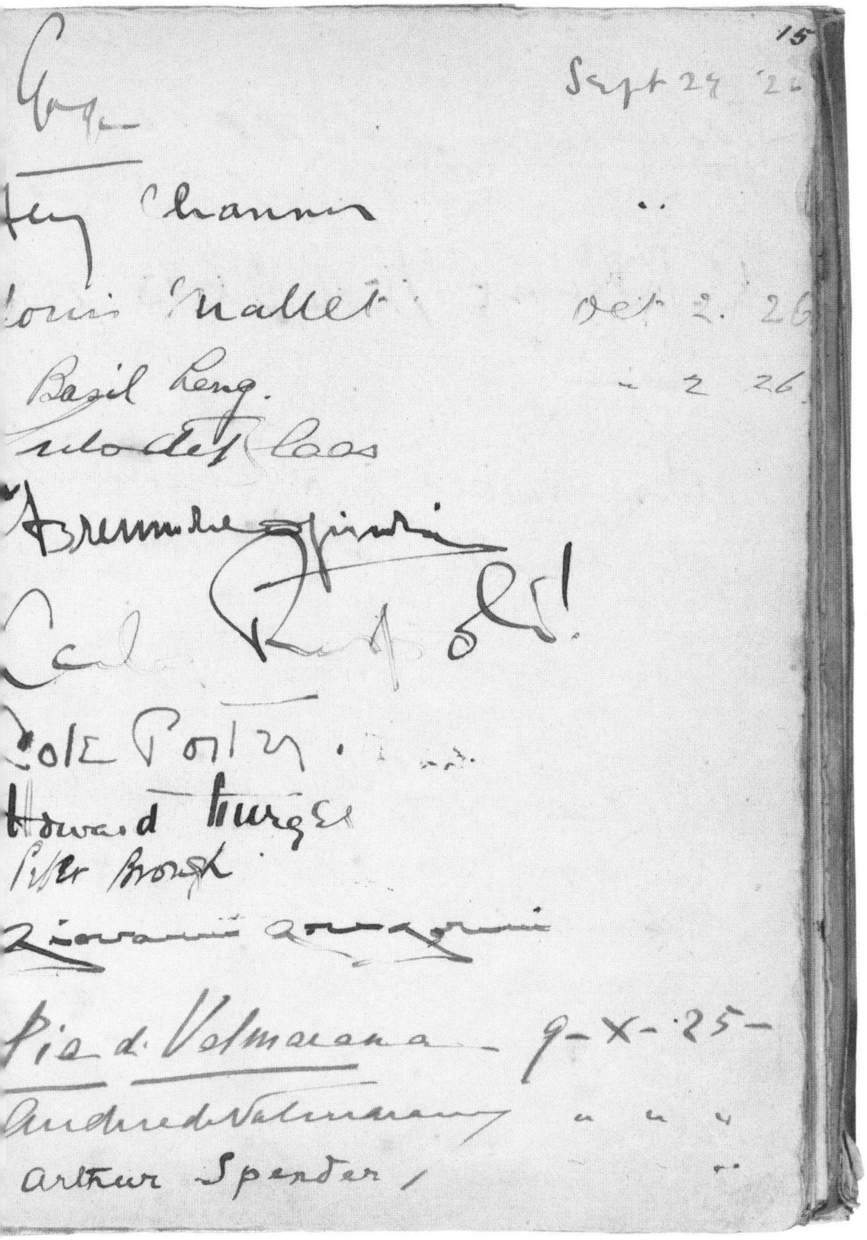

George

Sept 24 '26

Guy Channon

Louis Mallet   Oct 2. 26

Basil Leng.   ~ 2 26.

Carlo de Klaas

Brunn de Spirati

Carl Rudolf!

Cole Porter.

Howard Sturges

Peter Brough

Giovanni Comani

Pia di Valmarana ___ 9 - X - 25 -

André di Valmarana   " " "

Arthur Spender /

Signatures in the visitors' book: Ettore Tito, Giuseppe Volpi, and others, October 23, 1926, p. 16; Paul Morand, July 20, 1927; Serge Lifar, Serge Diaghilev, and others, August 8, 1927, p. 17

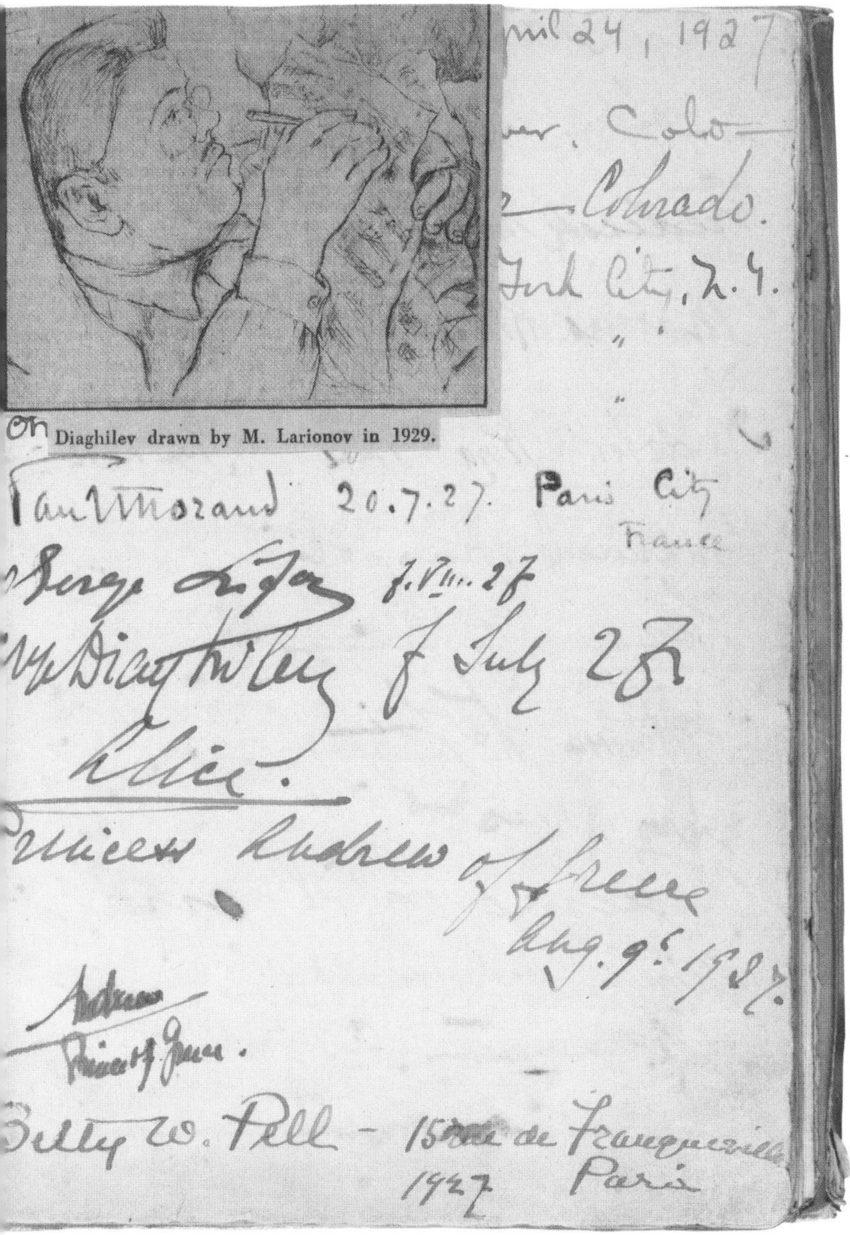

Diaghilev drawn by M. Larionov in 1929.

April 24, 1927

[various signatures and handwritten notes]

Paul Morand 20.7.27. Paris City
France

Serge Lifar 1.VIII.27

Serge Diaghilev 9 July 27

Alice

Princess Andrew of Greece
Aug. 9th 1927.

Andrew
Prince of Greece.

Billy W. Pell — 15bis de Franqueville
1927 Paris

Signatures in the visitors' book: Emilio Terry, Winston Churchill, Clementine Churchill, Diana Churchill, F.A. Lindemann, and others, October 1927, p. 23; Cecil Beaton and others, August 1929, p. 33

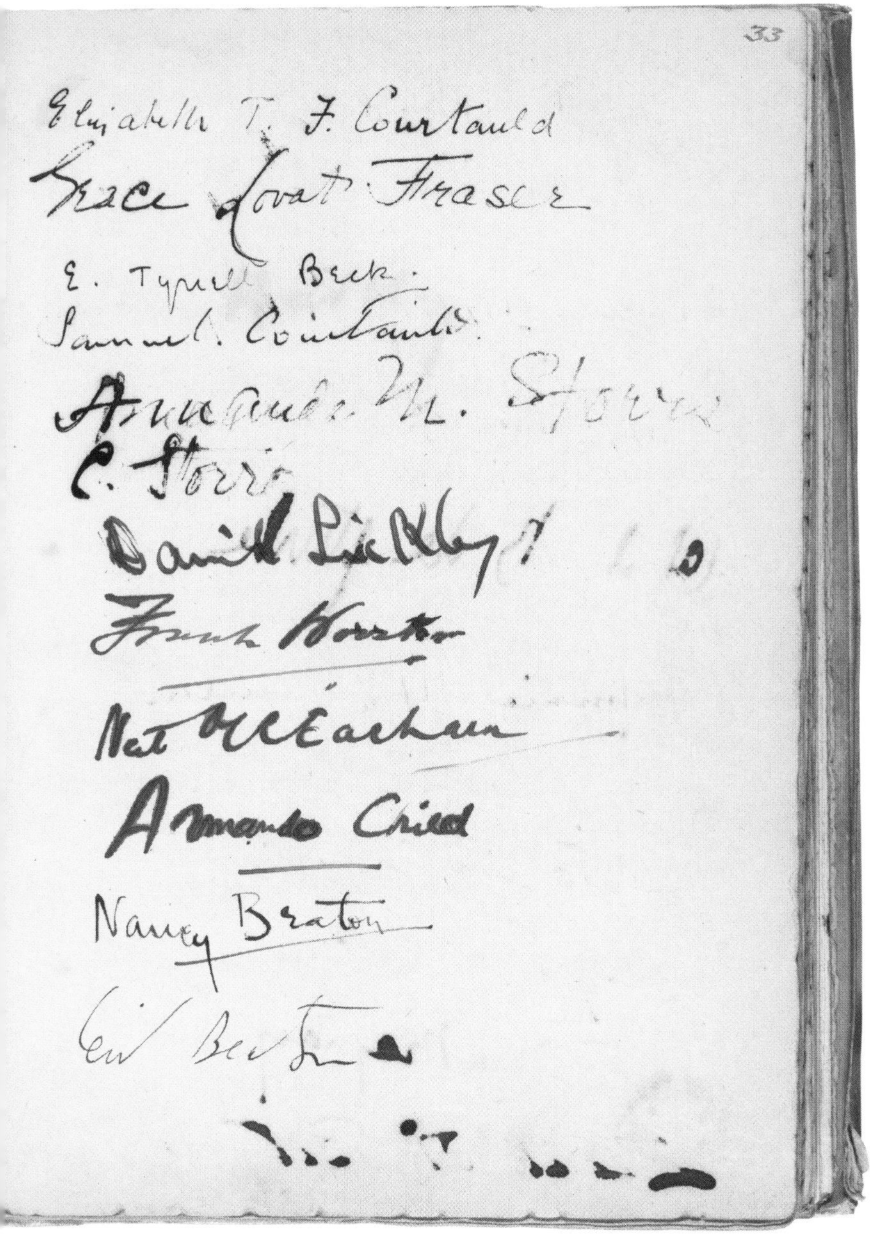

Elizabeth T. F. Courtauld

Grace Lovat Fraser

E. Tyrell Beck.

Samuel Courtauld.

Alexander M. Storrs

C. Storrs

David Pickley?

Frank Worston

Nat McEachun

A. mando Child

Nancy Beaton

Cecil Beaton

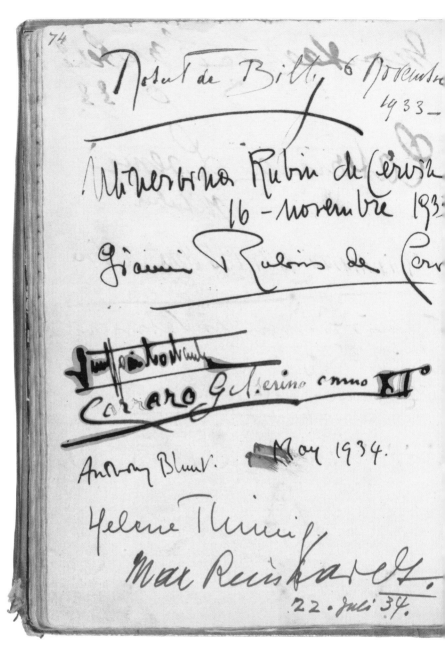

Signatures in the visitors' book: Anthony Blunt and others, May 1934, p. 74;
Le Corbusier, Caio de Mello Franco, and others, July 29, 1934, p. 75

Cecil Harcourt Smith. 29 July 1934.

Eric Maclagan.

Lea Corbusier

Caio de Mello Franco.
29 de Julho de 1934.

Raymond Harcourt Smith.
Simon Harcourt - Smith.

D. C. Bonner di Calvatone

Elsa Haldane.

Tono Puccirini
G. Charlot Harcourt.

Gary Baker.

183

On Sept 26ᵗʰ 1939 A. C. L. sailed
for Rio de Janeiro, Brazil.
On March 20ᵗʰ 1940 he married
Dorothea Mauran Watts, of
Newport Rhode Island, where they
lived until 1942, from when
their residence has been Sharon,
Connecticut. They only returned
to a war-battered & dilapidated
Malcontenta on Wed. April 23ʳᵈ 194̸7

Bertie Landsberg

Dorothea M. Landsberg —

During the war years, from
1939 to 1945, the villa & its
dependencies were occupied by
Germans, South African, British
and American troops.
Thirty one bombs fell in a semi-
-circle to the West & West-by-South
of the mansion, sinking two large
barges carrying & cargoes of wheat, & sand
but, fortunately, killing nobody.
5 Bombed-out Italian families (24 people)
lived in the house from Jan 1944 to
Oct 1ˢᵗ 1947. Among these were
april 11ᵗʰ 1947.

P.T.O

The return to La Malcontenta, visitors' book, April 23, 1947, pp. 113, 114

184

James Wir

Maria Hella Petrisson Wirz
thanks to whose persuasion of an
Italo-German "military-artistic mis-
-sion" the villa & its frescoes were
spared.

Alessandro Alessandri

our lawyer
should also be gratefully remem
-bered, as well as

Antonio Teolato . our former
& his good wife   Adele
who likewise were instrumental
in saving the villa, the former
losing a leg in faithful service.
On April 2th the Germans placed
31 bombs under the bridge in the
village. These by order of the "paroco"
S. Desiderio Barbato, parco   by the partisans
were removed & hidden near the vicarage
The "Boches" duly returned on the 5th to blow
up the bridge. Finding the bombs removed
they searched the whole village - including
the vicarage - but, fortunately, failed to
find them.
The British arrived on April 28th 1945.   about June 10th
George Corbr.   Thank God !

POST SCRIPTUM

My grandmother, nonna Elisabetta, showed no sign of having heard the siren.

The other women working in the house—there were three, all called Maria—had rushed out, as if the building itself had shaken them out of it. They ran to a dark, damp, centuries-old chamber, dimly lit from a hole in the ceiling. (It was one of those *caneve* [ice houses], which could be found in almost every villa built by Venetians in the past and which were used to store the winter ice so that, during the summer, it could be used to make the ever-fashionable lemon sorbets.)

My grandmother gently put down the book she was holding, but not without having first placed a bookmark on the open page. Taking her time, she rose to her feet, those chubby feet that tended to bulge slightly over the tops of her shoes, and—almost taking it for granted that I would be beside her— she said, "Let's go."

We left the frescoed room, decorated with a mythological scene that intrigued me because it included a stag (for what reason I was not sure), and we went carefully down a few steps and looked out over the lawn at the back of the house. There was absolutely no sign of the maids. The only faces I could see were those of the classical gods and goddesses, who regarded us with benevolence. We set off across the garden.

However, we had not yet reached the "air raid shelter" when the air filled once again with the scream of the siren, now signalling the "all clear."

Walking slowly beside my grandmother along the avenue of hornbeams (and picking up the small branches that had fallen across the path, because when dried they were useful kindling for the fire), I learned to distinguish between the noise made by reconnaissance aircraft and the roar of the four-engined bombers. I even saw the bombs leaving their bays and, after spinning a few times in the air, finding their trim as they hurtled towards the earth.

When my father, who was an engineer, came home— which was not every evening—he would ask me on which side the bombs had fallen: "behind the *barchessa*,"[96] "behind the Nalettos' house," "on the far side of the Pionca," or "on the other bank of the Brenta."

1944

Neither he nor his mother stopped to wonder, even for an instant, whether there might be a connection between the bombs and any form of apprehension on my behalf.

In this way I, too, learned not to be frightened. For example, from my place at table, I could look straight out of a large window. It was from there that once, even before hearing the explosion, I watched as the roof of a little cottage, perhaps only a hundred meters or so away from the house—on the far side of the Pionca, the canal that ran down the western edge of the garden—flew into the air and then disintegrated while still twenty or more meters above the ground.

Maria—one of the three—was holding a soup tureen in her trembling hands. My grandmother noticed that Maria was not wearing white gloves, as was expected while serving at table, without turning her head to see what had happened outside, she said in a calm, yet reproaching voice, but not without reproof, "Maria, what about your gloves?" Poor Maria answered, in a barely audible voice, "But, Countess, what about the bomb?" To which my grandmother replied, "Maria, you must explain what connection there could possibly be between your gloves and a bomb."

All that my father had to say about bombs was, "I have to run after bombs." Indeed, he hurried to the power stations as soon as these were hit by the Allied aircraft because it was his job to ensure the continued supply of electricity throughout that vast region, which was then called "Le Tre Venezie" (Venezia Giulia, Venezia Euganea, and Venezia Tridentina, covering most of north-east Italy from Alto Adige to Friuli, and parts of what are now Slovenia and Croatia). Then he added, "It's not a dangerous job. We are the same as bishops who are always the first to arrive at the site of the disaster; by then the bombers have moved somewhere else."

However, if I told my father that the bombs had fallen quite far away, "behind the *barchessa*" (namely to the east of my grandmother's house) my father would hesitate for a fraction of a second. "Was there an explosion?" he asked, fearing that a bomb might have hit the "powder magazine" at La Malcontenta. No, no explosion. "Well, let's go and see, all the same."

We went by bicycle. The family no longer had a car, apart from the "official" one, which in any case my father would never

Dear Anne:

This is the German sign from
MALCONTENTA. I took it down
from the wall myself. The man
who signed it is now in our hands
in Italy and is being questioned.
As I cannot be sure that Bertie lives
at SHARON, Conn. (my memory plays such
tricks) would you be kind enough
to forward it on to him with my
compliments. Thanks.

Bauwerk

mit seiner gesamten

Ausstattung

steht als

Kunstdenkmal

unter deutschem Schutz!

Belegung verboten!!

Bevollm. General d. Dtsch. Wehrmacht in Italien

Chef der Militärverwaltung

Abteilung Kunst-Archiv- und

Bibliothekschutz   gez. **K e s s e l r i n g**
                                      Generalfeldmarschall

MV-Abteilungs Chef

Protection order for La Malcontenta and its appurtenances, signed by General Field
Marshal Kesselring with a note by the person who sent this document to the Phillimores
after the end of the war

have even started unless he had been on duty. Our family car had been destroyed by a bomb, which fell in the garden of the house where we used to live in Padua, in Via Altinate, during a bomb attack that had filled the sky with fluttering scraps of burnt paper. As a result of that bombing, which had destroyed a good number of houses around us, we had to move to Mira, to a place called La Riscossa, where my grandmother's beautiful villa stood overlooking the Riviera del Brenta.

The bicycle leaned against the wall, under the portico of the *barchessa*, close to the gardener's lodgings. In homage to the profession, which he practiced with great zeal, the gardener had called his three children Narciso, Ortensia, and Violetta (Narcissus, Hortensia and Violet).

Ferrigo (I often called my father by his first name) helped me to climb onto the "bar"—the crossbar between the saddle and the handlebars on a men's bicycle—and we would set off slowly, following the course of the Riviera, along the tracks of the tram which at the time was known as the "brown cow": I don't know why.

At Oriago we crossed onto the opposite side of the canal, still going at a sedate speed. After quarter of an hour or so, we turned into a short avenue of mulberry trees—we called them *moreri* then, so we would be understood—which ended in a farmyard in front of another *barchessa*, more simple in appearance and less ornate than the one flanking grandmother's house at La Riscossa.

Ferrigo—true to his orderly nature—would never have gone through the gate on the other side of the yard without asking the custodian for permission. When Teodato appeared a few seconds later, there followed an extremely short exchange, mostly in the form of gestures. "Any problems?" "No, nothing serious."

Then they started off on a silent inspection of the grounds, ending with a stroll around a building that was severe, compact in shape, and rather unusual. My father stood looking at it—or, to be more precise, scrutinising it intensely. "Good."

The whole exercise seemed like a ritual. But Ferrigo never once told me that that house was a masterpiece of Italian Renaissance architecture, that it was the work of a great

architect of world renown, and that it had been built for his
forebears, who were therefore by definition also mine.
"It's important that it's not damaged," he used to say, without
giving any reason that might have helped to explain why.
In the meantime, without realising it, I took it all in.
The only thing he did say one day, when I was looking particularly puzzled, was no less enigmatic than the large building
around which we were slowly walking. "It's the house
of a gentleman who is no longer here. He cannot live here.
But he'll come back. And when he does come back, he must
find everything in order."

Then he would help me back onto the crossbar of the
bicycle and, in silence, we started making our way back to
La Riscossa. My grandmother—revealing in this her family's
German origins—was a stickler for punctuality.

As soon as I was back, I ran into the kitchen, which was
the warmest and liveliest part of the house, partly due to the
three Marias' endless chatter.

Given the frequency of the bombing raids, our visits to
La Malcontenta continued at quite regular intervals for a year
or two, but there were no unwelcome surprises.

One Sunday I saw that the German Wehrmacht had been
quartered on the large lawn behind the building. It was this
rear façade that now seemed to me increasingly seductive,
due to the unfathomable mysteries enveloping it. Grandmother's
park had also been occupied by German soldiers, but all
that I can really remember is that they obeyed the orders she
issued—which were spoken in short phrases with an impeccable German accent—without batting an eyelid.

On that occasion, Ferrigo was only concerned that a
sheet of paper should be securely attached to the main door
of the house, after the wind had almost blown it off: it was
an announcement from **General Kesselring** that placed the
monument under the protection of the Third Reich.

The Wehrmacht left La Malcontenta a little sooner than
the SS troops decamped from my grandmother's house.
I do not remember the exact dates, but I can still hear the songs
of the German soldiers, seated around a large bonfire at the
bottom of the park on the night before they left. And also—
perhaps ten days later—seeing the same unit reappear, totally

exhausted, having marched some six hundred kilometers for no good reason.

A few days after that we heard the loud rumble of a column of Allied tanks heading in an orderly fashion towards Venice. My mother helped me up onto the first tank. I held two tulips in my hands.

A New Zealander whose smile I will never forget gave me a bar of chocolate. I had not heard the word "chocolate" before, and so I thought that it, too, might be an explosive. I was too embarrassed to eat the bar, and this made all the soldiers on the tank laugh.

In my memory that tank then suddenly vanished in a blinding flash, perhaps just two hundred meters ahead of the spot where I had climbed off it. A few German soldiers had remained behind, crouching in the bushes, and they scored a direct hit with a bazooka. The column of tanks swung slowly and almost simultaneously fired perhaps a hundred shots in less than a minute. The next day, a bishop was also seen peering into the vast crater that now filled the site where the bushes had been.

All I can remember of the rest of the Allied occupation is an incident in which my grandmother, disgusted by a British officer who systematically ignored her instructions, ordered her car to be made ready (something I had never seen happen) and drove to the British HQ. She insisted that the official should be demoted and placed at her service for a few weeks as a simple soldier.

I have no other memories of trips to La Malcontenta, sitting on the crossbar of my father's bike, because there was no longer any reason for them. Now that the Allies were in Venice, the bombs that fell at La Malcontenta were dropped by their airplanes, but their targets were the industrial area around Marghera and the railway junction at Mestre.

Owing to its isolation in the middle of the flat countryside around Venice, its size, and the whiteness of its form, Palladio's villa on the banks of the Brenta was used as the reference point, marked on the Allied aircraft maps to indicate where the planes should start to release their bombs.

———

With the arrival of the Allies my memories of La Malcontenta were stored away in some remote recess of my mind.

1947

It wasn't that I didn't want to remember it, but just that there was no reason to refresh those earlier memories. At the age of five I started school and I had plenty of new things to do: in particular, I had to learn to get on with other children other than my brother. Then in 1947—precisely the year when Bertie returned to Italy and came back to La Malcontenta—Ferrigo, Teresa, Leonardo, and I, the whole family, moved to Venice. There were no more electric power stations to repair.

A much larger and more complex school than the one I had attended in Mira distracted me from the life I had lived up to then on the banks of the Brenta. Not to mention the freedom to walk around a city after spending my childhood in a park, which, however large, was still enclosed.

In the palace where we lived at first until my parents found a house, there was a large room filled with books on architecture; its crowning merit was that in the center stood a model of the Holy Sepulchre, and this alone absorbed any spare time that I had available.

When Bertie returned to La Malcontenta, he was not remiss in telephoning Ferrigo, to whom he was particularly grateful. However, it was a call that Ferrigo did not regard with pleasure. He did not like the fact that Bertie felt indebted to him for the care he had taken of the house during the war. To my father, that sort of care was an act he would have carried out, and would do so again, if it were necessary, out of a sense of moral duty. The grounds were quite simple: that house was a work of art; its owner would return and, when he did, he had to find it intact.

To Ferrigo, therefore, Bertie's gratitude seemed uncalled for and he found it embarrassing. Moreover, Ferrigo did not enjoy any occasion that he regarded as one of high society.

Yet so as not to appear discourteous, he did once accept an invitation to dinner at La Malcontenta, with Teresa, my mother. He returned very cheerful, having enjoyed himself thoroughly. A gentleman who had been seated next to him, having not heard him utter a word throughout the meal, turned to him at the end and, peeling an orange, said, "My dear friend, if silence is golden, you are a very rich man." When discussing that particular evening, I later heard Ferrigo comment how nice it was to meet intelligent people.

1948

Even the world surrounding my grandmother's villa had retreated a little into the past. However, it was vividly conjured up one day—this was in 1948—while I was watching a demonstration in Venice at which the participants, who were waving red flags, gave a rousing rendition of *Avanti popolo, alla riscossa*.[97]

To La Riscossa? That was exactly where my grandmother lived! "There may be too many of them to fit in the house," answered Ferrigo, in answer to my question. "If you want to see how many there are, you can come with me to Campo Santo Stefano tomorrow."

I knew the Campo well because I went to play there every day, yet when I saw it the following day I could never have imagined such a vast concourse of people.

My father and I were close to the monument. Since I was still a child, I couldn't see the stage on which the speaker had appeared, accompanied by great cheers from the crowds. "I can't see anything," I told my father. "It doesn't matter," he said. "Just listen." But I couldn't understand what Togliatti was talking about. "Notice his use of the subjunctive," Ferrigo told me. "Anyone who can use the subjunctive so well deserves to be listened to." I can still hear my father's voice as he said this.

I failed to understand the dangers of communism, in the same way I had failed to realize the danger of the bombings. I only knew that something extraordinary might happen during that dramatic year because of the determination with which Ferrigo refused to allow the owner of the beautiful house where, by then, we had gone to live, to remove the furniture and antique paintings and take them "abroad."

At what point I returned to La Malcontenta, and how, is something I don't remember. My only memory—and it may well have been on that occasion—is that I was enchanted by a girl, who was named after a precious stone, and who owned (or so I was told) a Palladian villa entirely decorated with frescos. I was deeply impressed by this information.

Then, once more, there is a blank period. A void, which, however, is comprehensible, because by then my life was filled with all the problems of adolescence, closely followed by those of school—namely the world.

1956

Not that I was very diligent at school, at least not until the last year of the classical lycée: the Marco Polo, which I attended in Venice. When I realized that I was about to sit an exam with external teachers—the so-called *esame di maturità* or baccalaureate—I began to work quite seriously. To my teachers' surprise I received a prize from the Ministry of Public Education for obtaining the highest marks of all the students in the province of Venice.

The question of which course to study at university never even crossed my mind then, in 1956, as I was revising for my exams. I had already reached that decision during the long, happy hours spent in the library, that wonderful room which contained a model of the Holy Sepulchre.

The choice of architecture, as the subject of my degree, brought me back, almost inevitably, to this masterpiece by Andrea Palladio, which stands, in imposing seclusion, on the right-hand bank of the Brenta. I used to go there with my companions from university and enjoy the welcome that I was offered, thanks to the kindness of the custodians who knew all about my father.

On each occasion my desire, and perhaps even my ability, to "read architecture" (as Bruno Zevi then said) grew stronger, but that particular building retained much of the mystery that I had experienced when, many years earlier, I first saw it, seated on the crossbar of my father's bike in a position that often made my right leg "go to sleep." The villa was a masterpiece that was waiting for someone. It earned my respect both for its loving devotion and its impeccable design.

However, I went no further than this, also because my "commitment"—or *impegno* as we called it in those days— did not allow room for any emotional distractions. (As well as my studies, I chaired the Students' Architectural Association of Venice, and I also edited the magazine *Venezia-Architettura*.)

However, I do remember one particular episode, which happened at this time.

I was coming back to Venice from Austria by train (it was a *littorina*, a diesel-powered railcar), seated in a compartment in which there were three young English women.

All of a sudden the conversation between the young women and the ticket inspector—who was speaking in Italian—

1957

grew louder; the English passengers didn't understand
why they were being asked to pay a surcharge. I thought I had
better intervene to calm things down, so I closed the book
I was reading and spoke to the young women in French (my
English was rather rusty).

One of the three—the quietest one—answered me, while
the other two looked completely blank, as if they were two dum-
mies. The misunderstanding was soon clarified. As I returned
to my book, I caught a quick exchange of looks between the
two women who had remained silent. Then they pulled a bottle
of raspberry grappa out of a basket, poured four fingers'
worth into a glass, and offered it to me, as if to say, "There, take
this, good man." I was very familiar with this Austrian grappa
and so, to their astonishment, I downed it in one and handed
back the glass. I never once looked up from my book
after that.

Only after we passed Treviso did the young woman who'd
already spoken to me ask, very politely, how she could reach
La Malcontenta. I suggested that she should get off the train at
Mestre and take a taxi; it was easier than going as far as Venice
and then taking the bus. I helped her with her suitcase when
she got off the train at Mestre and said, "Tell Bertie that Tonci
sends his regards." Then I returned to my seat on the train
and continued to travel to Venice, although the two women in
front of me seemed completely unaware of my presence.

The following day I received a telephone call from La Malcontenta at about nine a.m. "Mr Landsberg would be delighted
to invite you to lunch today." I thanked the caller and accepted.

At around midday, I boarded the direct bus for Malcontenta
from Piazzale Roma.

After a while—we had already passed Marghera—
I overheard a voice behind me, and recognized it as belonging
to the young woman who had offered me the grappa.
She was talking to an older man, who was sitting beside her.

When I glanced around to check if I was right, I distinctly
saw an expression of alarm on her face. Clearly she was
worried that I—the same man she had seen on the train the
day before—might be following her, or something.

She recovered from the surprise within a few minutes and,
with British phlegm and to sound out my intentions, she said,

"I'm going to Malcontenta." I replied, "So am I," in as laconic a tone of voice as I could manage. A couple of minutes passed and then she said, "I'm going to have lunch at a villa." "So am I," I answered, without even a trace of a smile. "How many villas are there in Malcontenta?" "One," I said.

When we got off the bus, she came up to me, almost cheerfully, and introduced me to her father, **Randolph Churchill**. She was **Arabella Churchill**.

Lunch was enjoyable, though my difficulties with the English language meant that I missed a few interesting and witty remarks. Bertie was very grateful for the help I had given his guest, and he was particularly pleased he would have a chance to greet my parents when I told him that I was accompanying them to a performance of Japanese Noh theater at the Teatro Verde on Isola di San Giorgio the following evening. He promised to come as well, provided that it did not rain.

Like Ferrigo and Teresa, and all those who came to that performance without knowing anything about the Noh tradition, I was so surprised by the mimicry, which was so different to our own—and interspersed with sharp blows and guttural sounds—that to my immense shame I couldn't help laughing and joining in the general hilarity.

It was while I had tears of laughter in my eyes that I distinctly remember seeing someone seated a few seats along from me, staring at me intensely and with amazement. It was the third young English woman whom I had met in the train and had not seen since.

Just two evenings later, she spotted me again at Palazzo Labia, that huge residence where, a few years earlier, **Carlos de Beistegui** had held a party, which had become famous all over the world. The dummy had come to life and now started to flirt outrageously with me, finding me ill-prepared and even a little prejudiced because I could not forget those incomprehensible red heels that I'd seen her wearing in the train, when she was sitting a few seats ahead of me.

Over the next few years, my contacts with the high-society world that Bertie invited to La Malcontenta were set in this mould: they were unpredictable and wholly eccentric compared to my own life at the time, which was regulated with a severity that now I regard as excessive. These events and situations

Arturo and Patricia Lopez-Willshaw; Diana Cooper as Cleopatra, Beistegui Ball, 1951
(photos: Cecil Beaton)

tended to repeat themselves almost mechanically, I thought,
unless I was willing to make a radical break.

But these invitations to La Malcontenta held a mysterious
attraction for me, and so I accepted another to dine there
a few days after we spent the evening at the Noh performance.
I arrived on time, on the usual bus, and found myself in the
company of individuals who did nothing to conceal their authority, however relaxed and light-hearted they were.

Lunch was served under the portico. Rust-colored sails—
an old set purchased from a Chioggia fishing boat—had been
hung from the columns to screen the magnificent table-setting
from curious passers-by. Bertie insisted that I should sit
at the head of the table. First he introduced the other guests,
who were all members of the British Cabinet gathered
around Randolph Churchill. He then introduced me, saying,
"This is the real owner of the house," and left.

It was not this introduction but rather my poor English
that prevented me from following the conversation among
the members of Her Majesty's Cabinet Office, which became
more strained as the minutes passed; Bertie's words certainly
gave me something to think about. I have never been a
"man of the world," at ease with games of this kind; yet, there
was also another reason. I knew—I can't remember how
I had found out, but I certainly knew—that, many years earlier,
Bertie had promised to give the villa to an English aristocrat.
This being the case, I wondered what had prompted him to say
those words.

I could only conclude that he had said them because this
superb architecture had been built by Palladio for the Foscari
brothers; therefore, on such a unique occasion, it was a brilliant
idea to place a Foscari at the head of the table, in the same
way that you might use a beautiful display of fruit as the center-
piece. However, many years later, I now realize that things were
not that simple.

Bertie's words had the effect of opening a window, and
allowing the breeze to blow aside a veil that otherwise I would
never have dreamed of lifting. However, the effect was very
short-lived, and any thoughts that may have stirred soon
subsided again, without really ever having reached my conscious
thoughts. I was wholly absorbed by my studies, to the extent

that at the beginning of September 1958—and I remember the occasion with a real sense of guilt—I refused an invitation to La Malcontenta, even though I knew I might have had a chance to meet **Igor Stravinsky** there.

Indeed, perhaps because of this feeling of reticence, I felt more comfortable going to La Malcontenta in winter, when the house was uninhabited and was used instead as a venue for university courses. I was delighted to accompany visiting professors (I remember **Bruno Zevi**'s visit, when he was working on his book on Palladio; **Carlo Scarpa**'s, too, was memorable because he walked slowly through the rooms, wondering where the best place was to sit, read, or draw at various times of day).

The *casa* was empty. Bertie and Dorothea used to leave in the fall—you might say they migrated—traveling to Sintra in Portugal, where they'd bought a house, Quinta de Capela, which they restored quite marvelously—or so everyone said. They spent the winter months there.

One year—it was 1961—Bertie telephoned from Portugal in early February. This had never happened before. "Tonci," he said, "please don't go to Malcontenta in May this year, or even in June." I was surprised. He may have thought I was offended. So he added, "I'll arrive in early July and I'll explain then." After a short pause, he continued, "I'll also let you in on a secret." When **Princess Margaret** and **Anthony Armstrong-Jones** arrived at La Malcontenta at the end of May, I thought this must have been the secret that I was supposed to keep. But instead the secret was eventually given to me in an envelope: it contained the copy of a letter to Bertie from **Peggy Guggenheim**, the great American collector, and Bertie's reply to her.

Apart from this one occasion, Bertie and Dorothea returned to La Malcontenta every year, in late spring, and resumed their life in the villa, following a ritual that, in its own way, was governed by strict rules.

Part of that ritual was the annual telephone call to my father, who regularly turned down the invitation to visit. I was then invited in his place, accepting in the knowledge that the pursuant hours would be very different to my normal routine.

Once I sat next to a Russian princess whose face was so pale that I thought she had emerged straight from a catacomb;

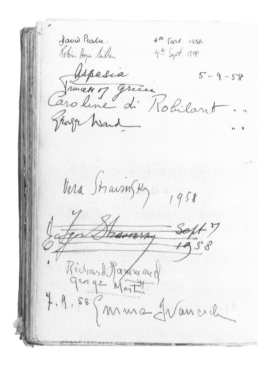

Igor Stravinsky with Vera and Robert Craft in Venice (photo: Gjon Mili)
Igor Stravinsky's signature in the visitors' book, September 7, 1958

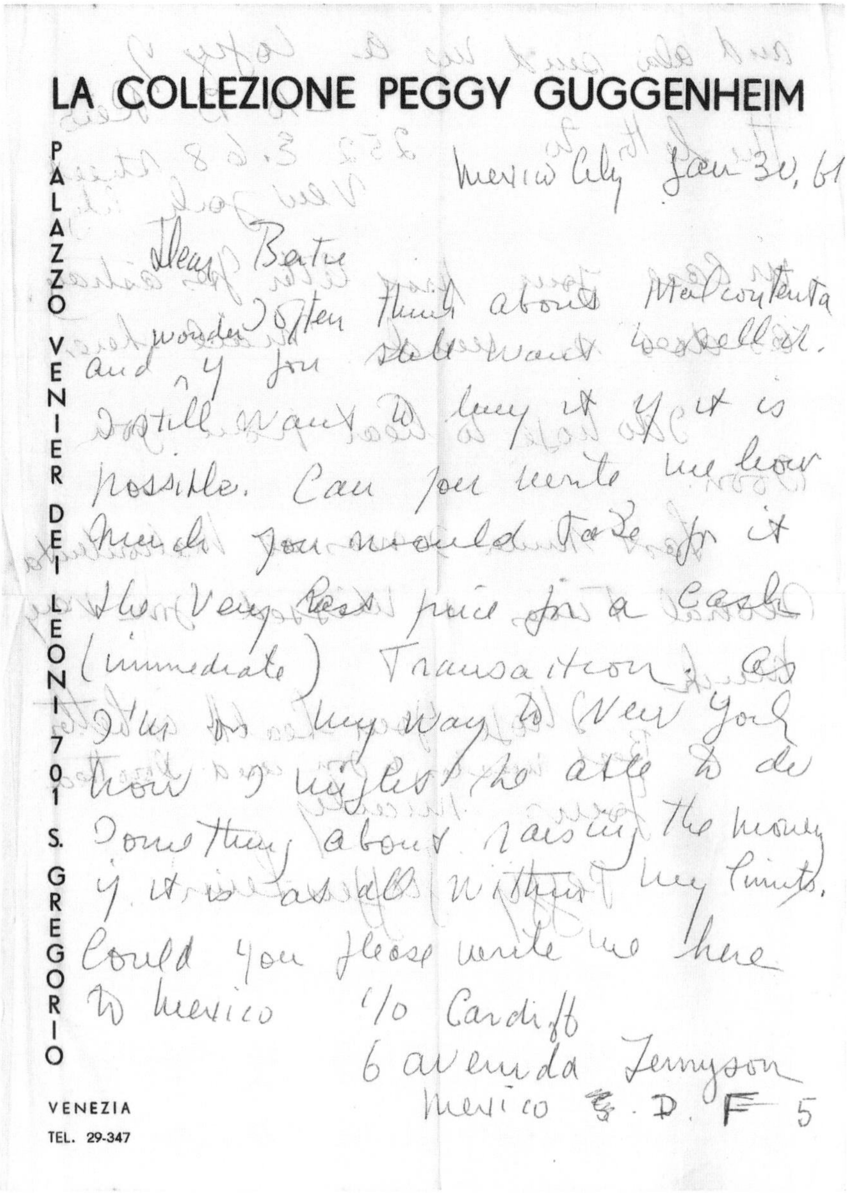

LA COLLEZIONE PEGGY GUGGENHEIM

PALAZZO VENIER DEI LEONI 701 S. GREGORIO

VENEZIA

TEL. 29-347

Mexico City Jan 30, 61

Dear Bertie

I often think about Malcontenta and wonder if you still want to sell it. I still want to buy it if it is possible. Can you write me how much you would take for it the very last price for a cash (immediate) Transaction. As I'm on my way to New York now I might be able to do something about raising the money if it is at all within my limits. Could you please write me here to Mexico c/o Cardiff 6 avenida Tennyson Mexico D. F. 5

Peggy Guggenheim, letter to Bertie Landsberg, January 30, 1961

"Dear Bertie, I often think about Malcontenta and wonder if you shall want to sell it. I still want to buy it if it is possible. Can you write me how much you would take for it, the very last price for a cash (immediate) transaction. As I'm on my way to New York now I might be able to do something about raising the money if it is at all within my limits. [...] Yours sincerely, Peggy Guggenheim"

Peggy Guggenheim at
the Palazzo Venier dei Leoni,
Venice 1961

Bertie Landsberg, letter to
Peggy Guggenheim, February 12, 1961

"Dear Peggy,
It was pleasant to hear from you, although
whenever anyone approaches me in

connection with my, possibly, selling
Malcontenta I realize how loath I would
be to do so! After all, it is—not only in
my own opinion but also in that of such
others as Sir Kenneth Clark, etc.: 'the most
beautiful house in the world.' Its value,

as just land and 'buildings' has been rising by leaps and bounds, but, of course, its chief worth is as a very great work of art and one of the recognized masterpieces of architecture of the world. As such, its worth is inestimable. But I need not say all this to you. [...]

Yours sincerely,
Bertie Landsberg"

she insisted that I listen to her and look straight into her eyes, which might once, perhaps, have been beautiful. On another occasion, I was seated next to an elderly Venetian aristocrat, who amazed me because he was guzzling cherries (the wild sort which **Maria Besa**, the housekeeper, referred to in her unmistakeably nasal accent as *duraccine*), yet he never spat out a single stone.

"You see that woman," he said, pointing at his wife (the same Mrs Lee who had bought the famous production of textiles that had belonged to Mariano Fortuny, and who had married my neighbor so she felt more Venetian). "She would like me somehow to get the stones from my mouth onto a fork and then from my fork onto the plate. It's too complicated, so I just swallow them."

At the end of the dinner—I think it was this one—Bertie presented me with a fragment of the bell, which used to be on top of the house; it was a piece of bronze embedded in the beam that used to support it. "It's yours," he said. On seeing my hesitation, and my uncertainty about receiving a gift, he added, "It's always been yours."

These words, although brief, were voiced with a certain amount of difficulty, almost of suffering. Bertie's face was often slightly flushed and clammy, and he breathed heavily when speaking. These things, which I had forgotten, came clearly back to mind many years later, when I was talking to **Joseph Brodsky**: he also had quite long hair, although it was sparse, leaving the top of his head quite bald; he also perspired slightly, and his voice seemed to struggle, as if against some inner sorrow.

Though suffering from a weak heart, Bertie always came down the narrow spiral staircase from the first to the ground floor, bidding his guests farewell from the front door.

It was here, between the two large vases of sweet jasmine, in the fall of 1964, that Bertie told me, "I would like you to visit the house occasionally, when I'm not here."

I thought that this was just a polite thing to say, a way of behaving that came naturally to him.

It is difficult to remember exactly, but I believe my visits to La Malcontenta were no more frequent than in previous years: that is to say, I went every now and again. Or perhaps

I went even less: the reason was that I met **Barbara** that winter, and—whenever I was not at work—she was uppermost in my thoughts. I did not involve her in the preparation of the exhibition of drawings for the new hospital in Venice, which was being held to mark Le Corbusier's visit to Venice. However, she and I dined with **Le Corbusier** on a number of pleasant evenings in April while he was in Venice. I still remember, with emotion, how delighted the grand old man—who had refused to speak publicly during his visit—was to be in Barbara's company. When we left the restaurant, he held her arm and talked on and on; these long monologues were a gift reserved solely for her ears.

It was only later that summer that I realized I hadn't received my usual invitation to lunch on the banks of the Riviera. It was then that I understood, without being told, that Bertie was dead. I have to say that I felt I had wronged him, because I had never accepted his invitation to visit Sintra, in that enchanting spot he had chosen—as he had chosen Venice, as a young man—"following in Byron's footsteps."

Dorothea came alone to La Malcontenta the following year. She was a tidy person, self-contained, and perhaps a little severe to look at. Until then, I had never really got to know her and, if truth be told, I never did, even afterwards.

My difficulties with English did not help, nor did her markedly American accent. I was embarrassed by the linguistic barrier. But, above all, to me Bertie had always been the soul of this house, because he loved it as one might love an idea, or a utopia. He looked at the architecture, the frescos, and the objects in a way that prompted you to look at them as you never otherwise would have, and to understand them. Without any lectures.

Bertie loved conversation, not lectures.

He kept two large books, open, on the table in the center of the large central chamber. In it he had arranged prints, images, newspaper cuttings, letters: anything that concerned the house, or the King of France who had stayed here. These books served as a sort of handbook, which he would leaf through in order to entertain his visitors. However, whenever a professor walked in—a category of individuals for whom he expressed very little enthusiasm—he would walk over to the

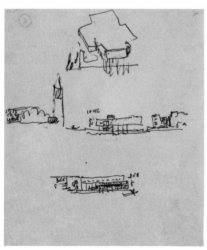

Le Corbusier, Antonio Foscari (behind), and others at the inauguration
of the exhibition of the project for Venice's new hospital, April 12, 1965
Le Corbusier in Venice, in front of the *Scuola* of San Marco, 1964
Le Corbusier, sketch of the church of San Marco and the new hospital in Venice, 1964

table and deliberately close the books. He didn't want these professors to discover his amateur approach so easily.

Later that fall I received a telephone call from Dorothea, inviting me to lunch. When I arrived, I walked around the house and up to the portico, as I always had done.

But I was invited to go downstairs to the ground floor. Dorothea was waiting for me to join her in the "old kitchen." The wood burning in the large fireplace gave off a pleasant smell. The table was set for three. Claud, **Claud Phillimore**— Dorothea pronounced the names clearly so I would understand—was not yet present, but he would not be long. He was living in the building known as Orto Chiuso, overlooking the large lawn "behind the house."

Without looking at me directly, Dorothy told me about the noble antecedents of the Phillimore family, about the architectural practice that Claud had established in London before the war, and how he and **Anne** had been married in Cairo and now had two children.

Dorothea spoke as if she felt obliged, in some way, to pass on this information, almost as if to break down the reserve that, until then, had always prevented her from asking me questions when she came to La Malcontenta. The very possibility of any familiarity between Bertie and myself was based on the understanding that I respected the cosmopolitan, aestheticizing and, in many ways, eccentric world to which he belonged, in every way, in the same way that he respected that sort of radicalism which he saw in myself, the somewhat provincial architecture student.

Although it might seem unlikely, neither Bertie nor I ever failed to respect this understanding when we met. It was on the basis of such mutual respect that, over the years, we grew to enjoy what I considered a real friendship.

While I was thinking of these things, Dorothea might well have continued her monologue, of which I had lost the thread some time ago, if Claud had not walked into the "old kitchen," almost slipping through its doors. For the first time, I saw the secret smile that always hovered around the corners of his mouth and eyes.

Suddenly I found myself overwhelmed by bursts of words, whose sense I gave up trying to follow, and by silences filled

with a sense of fascination that was difficult to gauge. I had
no other option but to concentrate on the taxing task of picking
the stray radicchio leaves off my plate, after I had finished the
hard-boiled eggs.

In order to establish a relationship with Dorothea and
Claud, I had to find solid ground on which to intervene.
Furthermore, this was my only chance to restore, and perhaps
even to reinvigorate, the totally abstract bond between
myself and this house.

As I walked out of the "old kitchen" after lunch that day,
it suddenly came to me that I could attempt a difficult enterprise:
I could reinstate the fresco—a depiction of an ideal *Concerto*,
then housed in the Civic Museum of Verona—which had been
detached from the wall of the square room, on the west side
of the *piano nobile*, using a technique known as *strappo* (taking
a transfer of an image).

I contacted **Licisco Magagnato**, the director of Verona's
museums, that same day, I think. I had met him a few times
when I accompanied Carlo Scarpa to Verona while he was
overseeing the restoration of Castelvecchio. I put this astonishing request to Magagnato.

He listened to my proposal—and to my supporting
arguments that this "strappo" technique was now prohibited
in Italy and that, therefore, the restoration of the painting
cycle in this Palladian building would be an excellent cultural
precedent—with growing amazement and alarm. However,
I didn't press my case because, literally while I was talking to
Magagnato, I remembered—vaguely at first, and then quite
distinctly—that Bertie had told me about other fresco transfers
that he had seen, or perhaps had even had in his possession
and then lost. It was this clue that sent me hurrying in a different direction.

As soon as I saw them again, I asked Dorothea and Claud
about these fresco transfers. They knew nothing and so
I requested their permission to search the villa, Orto Chiuso,
the *barchessa*, and the adjacent buildings.

With their agreement, I set off for the *barchessa*; I have
forgotten the exact details and I think, in my excitement, I was
acting like an automaton. I climbed to the upper floor, which
was formerly a granary, and there, in a corner of this vast space

filled with all manner of objects, I saw some clumsily rolled bundles of jute cloth with faint traces of color on their inner surfaces.

Dorothea and Claud were on the point of leaving La Malcontenta, after what had been only a short visit, and so I hurriedly asked them to allow me to look into this "discovery."

That winter I brought these frayed cloths to Venice and the following spring I was able to return to La Malcontenta with the carefully stretched canvases preserving as much as possible of the frescos, ripped from the walls a few decades earlier. Quite naturally, I was impatient to see Dorothea's reaction. I asked her to let me know when she planned to return to the villa, so I could be there when she first saw this surprising new development. I distinctly recall my sense of expectation when she entered the room, but she walked slowly through it without interrupting the narrative of a trip she had just finished. With a certain degree of caution, she crossed over to the door on the opposite side of the room and walked out without saying a word.

I, too, said nothing. However, I did feel that she might at least have asked me where I had put the large tapestry and the large painting, both of which I had had to remove before replacing the restored frescos on the walls. Above all, I could not understand why she had said nothing about the frescos.

I decided to persist. After a short time, I found an excuse to return to the room, again with Dorothea. Taking courage, I said to her, "Do you like the frescos which I've managed to return to their rightful place?"

"How wonderful," said Dorothea. Then, turning her back to the wall with the newly restored frescos, she started to describe the figures that Giambattista Zelotti had painted four centuries earlier. My amazement was short-lived: I realized after a few instants that she was describing the fresco transfer, which she had seen and memorized when visiting the museum in Verona. The image on that fresco was still reversed, as the detached fresco had never been correctly remounted. Dorothea was blind, or very nearly so; as she walked, she could still make out the dark shapes of furniture and see the light shining from the door.

As I came to terms with this discovery, I was left with a strange sensation: now I had a clear responsibility to protect this house, which, for many reasons, I had come to love. Indeed, my life at the university, the architectural competitions that I was entering, and all my other commitments would never prevent me—or so I thought—from making frequent visits to La Malcontenta.

I didn't tell Dorothea about everything I did. To give just one example, I didn't tell her the lengths I had to go to in order to prevent the felling of the poplars, which Bertie had planted on the other bank of the Riviera to screen off Marghera's industrial sprawl. Over the years the trees had grown taller and thicker, but Dorothea would not have managed to see even the few poplars that I did manage to save, and she would have been saddened by the thought of those that had gone.

In the meantime the *casa*—this house on which Bertie had showered such love—was deteriorating at an alarming speed.

The fact that it was lived in only by an elderly lady who could not see the perfection of its architectural forms and the ideal use of pictorial decoration, let alone the dust accumulating on the furniture, undermined that notion of prophecy, and therefore hope, which are the quintessential features of this architecture.

Claud—who used to come to La Malcontenta during the summer—rang me only once in all these years. I dined with him on the ground floor of Orto Chiuso, served by "the merry maids" (as Claud used to call Ina, Ida, and the dark-haired Maria, all of whom often sang as they cooked and cleaned).

On that occasion, too—as at our first meeting—his smile, which was so difficult to define, his enigmatic way of waiting for an answer to a question that he had not even asked, and his direct gaze, which was never at all invasive, established a bond between us that was stronger than I had imagined. When Dorothea died, I rarely went to La Malcontenta; maybe I thought my contribution to the house was no longer required since I knew that Claud was an architect of infallible taste. Or perhaps there was some other reason.

This created a strange situation. When I met Claud—which happened probably once a year—we would sit together, almost without speaking, as if we had agreed on everything and therefore further talk was unnecessary.

Orto Chiuso, interior (photo: Lord Snowdon)
Anne, Miranda, Claud and Francis Phillimore, Dorothea and Bertie Landsberg
in the garden of La Malcontenta, 1951

The villa did not belong to me, except in a childhood dream
that had become a lucid abstraction. Claud was the owner,
but he behaved as if this were not the case—or rather as if the
house belonged to his past, to an ideal world that he could
only fully experience through memory. Whenever he came to
La Malcontenta, he used to stay at Orto Chiuso, with his wife and
children. He rarely invited guests to the villa. If he did so, they
were Bertie's old friends. Only on a few occasions did he sleep
in the large bed, with its slender columns topped with gilded
balls, in the room whose ceiling is decorated with the fresco
of Bacchus and Ariadne.

On one of these occasions he was woken in the night by
a scuffling noise, as he described it about ten years later when
we were sitting together on a warm fall day. When the thieves
entered the room, he had lain stock-still, with his eyes shut
and his body covered by only a sheet. A few seconds later,
a torch beam swung towards the bed. At that moment, Claud—
who was tall, thin, and moved with perfect coordination—
slowly sat up, with staring eyes. The thieves, convinced that the
house was empty, fled in terror, dropping all the loot that they
had amassed.

Claud frequently walked over to the large house at dawn,
which was his favorite time. He would sit in an armchair
close to the large window in the central room, and would read
or write in the notebook that he always carried with him. A smile
broke out on his face, as if the memories that came to mind
brought with them some form of satisfaction. He, like the house,
was poised between the past and the future, remembering
and waiting.

However, it was tacitly understood—perhaps because this
is what I had done while Dorothea was alive—that in his absence
I could come here, even stay in the villa if I wished to: I, who
had come here as a child; the young man whom Bertie had
invited once a year; the professional who had rediscovered the
frescos. This created a bond between us, one that was mysteri-
ously reinforced year after year, even though we hardly ever met.

One evening, as Barbara and I were talking after nearly
eight years of married life, we remarked on this enigma. It was
a puzzle, in the same way that the fate of this perfect house was
mysterious: it had been the object of such love, yet it had never

been fully owned by anyone. It had, one might say, remained a virgin, protected by the purity of its architectural form.

As we spoke about this mystery—or perhaps this miracle— Barbara said, "Why don't you talk to Claud about it? Give him a ring." It was clear what I had to do, and the time had come to do it.

"It's been a long time since you came to Malcontenta," I said to Claud. "It's been a long time since we talked. I feel that I need to talk to you about it. I feel concerned. I don't understand what I need to do, if indeed I need to do anything. What is the future of this masterpiece?"

"Say that again," whispered Claud.

"I don't know what to say, except that I need to talk to you. I need to understand. I need to know. Because this house is now in some way part of me. If you were ever to leave it, I would suffer. However, if you ever think about doing that, you must let me know. Because I would do anything to keep it for us: for you, for Barbara, and for the child that Barbara is now expecting."

I stopped to draw breath. I had said things that I had not planned to. These words came after such a long period of silence—blanketing my own thoughts—that they seemed unbalanced. Indeed, I was unbalanced, psychologically if nothing else.

Claud said nothing. His silence seemed interminable. I was frightened for a moment that I had said too much, that I had broken into a sanctuary.

"Claud, Claud," I said.

After another long pause, Claud said, "Tonci, I've waited for this phone call for eight years." Then he was silent again for a while before stating, "I sold the villa last week."

"Tonci, Tonci!" Now Claud needed to hear my voice. At this point, I had fallen into a daze and was completely paralyzed.

When I eventually managed to speak again, Claud told me that he would think about what I had said and would ring me back.

Throughout the entire conversation, Barbara and I sat together on our white sofa. When the conversation ended, we were left speechless and stunned. We did not know what to think. In fact, we didn't think of anything, and as far as I can remember even the next day we didn't talk about it.

Lord Snowdon, self portrait
Dorothea and Bertie Landsberg with Thai (photo: Lord Snowdon)

Maria Besa (photo: Lord Snowdon)

About a week later, or perhaps a little more, the phone rang. It was evening again. Claud's calm voice told me to get in touch with Paolo Magrini, his personal lawyer in Venice.

The lawyer told me things I had never known. That for many summers Anne, Claud's wife, used to come to La Malcontenta with Francis and Miranda, their wonderful children. They stayed at Orto Chiuso, that small villa which overlooked the large lawn in the park. Bertie used to visit them there. When Bertie died, it was Claud and Anne who used to visit Dorothea from time to time. Paolo Magrini told me all of this without emotion. Yet, as a passionate rower himself, his voice grew animated as he described, in some detail, how Anne and her children had learned to row a *sandolo* and to sail a *topo a vela* (a type of traditional Venetian sailing boat), which were moored in the small inlet beside the villa.

Then Magrini told me that Dorothea had never really accepted the fact that, prior to their marriage, Bertie had promised to gift the villa to Claud; and how, in her will, Dorothea had left a considerable sum of money to the University of Virginia so it could buy the villa off Claud.

A decision of this kind revealed a clearly American form of reasoning, but there was also another reason: namely, that the University of Virginia was founded by a fervent admirer of Palladio, Thomas Jefferson. However, until this moment, Claud had succeeded in evading the repeated approaches made by the university.

I left the lawyer's office, which was in the Corte dell'Albero, lost in my own thoughts. Once again, I had heard myself uttering words to the lawyer that I'd never thought I would say: I had told him that I was ready to match the university's offer, and that I would willingly keep the same conditions. This house had to be loved, I had thought, not used.

The lawyer reported this conversation to Claud, who rang me a few hours later. "Let's see," he said. There was a light-hearted tone in this brief expression. It was as if he were preparing himself to play a game.

Indeed, although Claud had signed the preliminary contract, he had not yet submitted his conditions to the university management, and these would have had to form an integral part of the final agreement.

Only later, after I had finalized my agreement with Claud through the Venetian lawyer, did I hear what Claud had done. With that imperturbable smile on his face all the while, he had stated his terms to the prospective American buyers: that the villa should never be subject to structural alterations nor changes to its internal layout; that no more sanitary fittings should be added; that no changes should be made to the color of the windows and doors; that there should be limited use of electric lighting throughout the building; and lastly, that the vases with lemon trees should be maintained in front of the south-facing façade.

As he gradually listed these conditions, adding another at every step, the buyers, who in their pragmatism had planned to use the Palladian complex as a summer residence for their students, took a step backwards. Finally, after a few weeks of embarrassed silence, the university decided that the property was not suitable for their purposes because they would not be able to use it as an educational facility, still less to provide accommodation for guests.

I must admit that when Claud told me this, I was about as dazed as I'd been when he told me that the villa had been sold. Never had I imagined that I might one day own a Palladian building, and I certainly had no idea of the scale of the commitment I was taking on.

I did have one instinctive reaction to set my own conditions. I asked that, even once the deed had been transferred, Claud should continue to regard this house as his own. In short, he should not abandon us. There was so much we needed to learn from him. Our actions (and I continue to use the first person plural here because all my feelings were completely shared by Barbara) had not been prompted by a desire for ownership, but rather by the conviction that the bond of love for this marvellous architecture—a bond that had started in 1924 when Bertie had rediscovered the house, decrepit, on the banks of the Riviera del Brenta—could not be interrupted.

As the legal formalities continued, I remember only that at some point these matters accelerated somewhat. While my mind was still in turmoil, the lawyer Magrini carefully started to explain that separate deeds had been drawn up for the transfer of the house, the lands, and for those movables which I had

Freya Stark at La Malcontenta (photos: Antonio Foscari)

Hanging the sails between the columns of the pronaos of La Malcontenta
(photo: Lord Snowdon)

Bertie Landsberg (photo: Lord Snowdon)

Barbara Foscari and Claud Phillimore (photo: Antonio Foscari)
Barbara (pregnant with Giulia) and Antonio Foscari, with Ferigo, their son, on the lawn
(photo: Mauro Galligani)

expressed interest in buying. I remember the delicacy and prudence with which the lawyer informed me that Claud did not want the house to be the object of a contract of sale, since this would have minimized its moral value and in some way contaminated the concept of its beauty. Nothing could have been more agreeable to my state of mind.

Claud was due to arrive from London in mid-December to discuss the furniture.

We arranged to meet at La Malcontenta. He was already there when I arrived. As I climbed the spiral staircase to the first floor, I heard regular thuds coming from above. I stopped on the landing, wondering what was going on. Then Claud appeared on the stairs, dragging a heavy bag. I looked at him. He smiled. "It's a corpse," he said.

The bag was full of books, just a tiny part of the mountain of books with which Bertie had whiled away his time here, when he was not busy entertaining his guests.

Leaving the bag on the landing, Claud led the way into the large cross-shaped hall, which, at that moment, was illuminated by the low sun whose rays shone directly into the far northern end of the chamber. We looked at the room as if neither of us had ever seen it before.

"It's perfect," I said, after a while. There was a long pause, and then Claud repeated, "Yes, it's perfect."

A few days later, Claud, the lawyer, the first-rate notary who then lived in Mira, Barbara, and I all met, as arranged, in St Mark's Square in Venice. It was quite late in the evening. We found a café whose staff kindly agreed to let us enter, even though it was past closing time.

In slow cadenced tones, Alberto Tessiore, the notary, read all the clauses, one after the other, of the contract for the sale of the grounds and the donation of the villa. Barbara and I listened, filled with emotion and well aware that this was an event that would affect our future in so many ways. Claud smiled and, as the reading progressed, he remarked on the length of the legal document, with a dramatic gesture mimicking the slow unrolling of a long scroll of paper.

———

1974

A few days later—the large meadow was sparkling with hoar frost—we went to La Malcontenta with Claud. Both Barbara and I wanted him to open the door and welcome us in. Instead there was a moment of hesitation on the threshold about who should go first: who was the guest, and who the host?

Once inside, Barbara and I walked around carefully, almost hesitantly, as if Bertie or Dorothea, or even their little dog that was always at their heels, might walk through one or other doorway.

"On we go," said Claud.

"Why don't you stay?" I replied.

"I'll be back in May."

True enough, he was. "Now that it's your house, and I'm a guest, I feel quite happy sleeping here."
He chose the mezzanine room on the east side, which has been known ever since as Claud's room.
Barbara and I have always believed that it is important to preserve—and defend—this continuity. That is why we asked Irma, the imposing housekeeper who knew Bertie and Dorothea, to offer a particularly warm welcome to any visitors— among the many that come to admire Palladio's architecture—whom she recognized as their friends. Above all, we asked her to offer them vermouth, which Bertie always served to his guests, and even to leave them alone in the house (if they wished to stay) when Barbara and I were absent. We asked Maria, Ina, and Ida, the "merry maids," to help in the villa so that Claud would hear the same voices and the same songs that had delighted him when he stayed at Orto Chiuso.

That year, Claud arrived at La Malcontenta in early May. He settled into his room and waited for Barbara and me to join him. When we arrived in early June, we brought with us Ferigo, who had been born on May 20.

Andy Warhol, Venice, September 12–17, 1977

The two central sections of this contact sheet include photographs of Villa Foscari La Malcontenta taken by Andy Warhol. The photograph marked in red pencil shows Andy Warhol at La Malcontenta with Douglas Christmas of ACE Gallery, the curator of Warhol's exhibition *Torsos*, which opened at the Prigioni Vecchie in Venice in occasion of Warhol's Venetian trip.

Antonio Foscari to Andy Warhol: "Tell me, do you like this architecture?" Andy Warhol to Antonio Foscari: "I can't say. I haven't developed the photos yet."

226

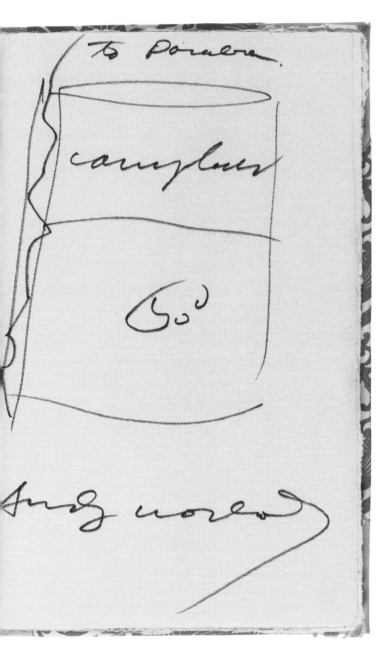

Andy Warhol, *Campbell*, with dedication "To Barbara," visitors' book, p. 13

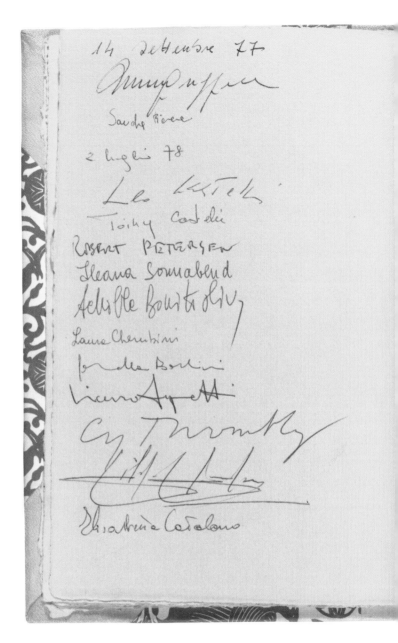

Signatures in the visitors' book: Leo Castelli, Ileana Sonnabend, Cy Twombly, and others, July 2, 1978, p. 14

Leo Castelli and Cy Twombly at La Malcontenta, July 2, 1978

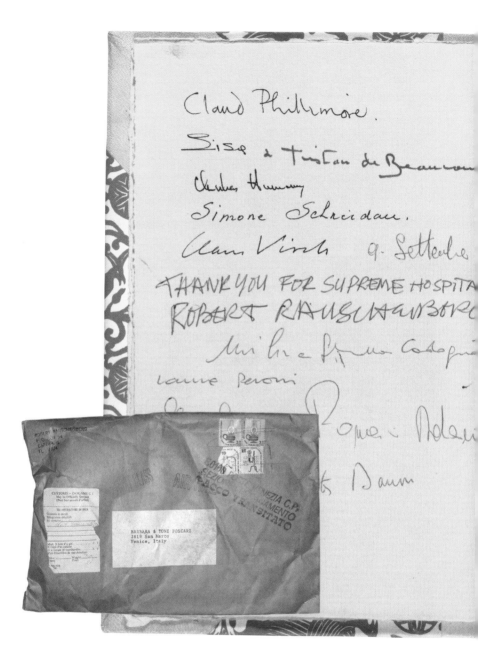

Message by Robert Rauschenberg in visitors' book, September 9, 1975, p. 8, and unopened package containing "Hot Sauce" sent later by Rauschenberg to Barbara and Antonio Foscari

FOR TONCI + BARBARA —BOBRAUSCHENBERG—74

Photo sent by Robert Rauschenberg to Barbara and Antonio Foscari in allusion to the
external stairs of La Malcontenta, with dedication "For Tonci + Barbara," 1979

Jean Tinguely, preparatory drawings for the sculpture realized at La Malcontenta, 1987

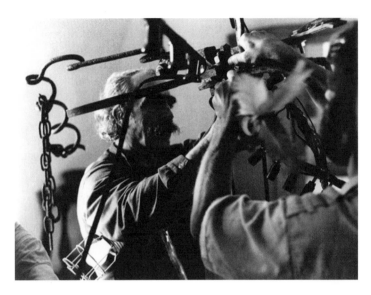

Jean Tinguely working on his sculpture; Antonio Foscari and Jean Tinguely,
La Malcontenta 1987 (photos: Leonardo Bezzola)

233

Jannis Kounellis with Antonio and Barbara Foscari looking at Kounellis' sculpture in the room of Prometheus; Jannis Kounellis at La Malcontenta, 1992 (photos: Claudio Franzin)

Jannis Kounellis and Barbara Foscari in the pronaos of La Malcontenta, 1992
(photo: Claudio Franzin)

Notes

1 Paul's father, Peter Rodocanachi—who was brought up as a Christian, in the Greek Orthodox church—had moved to London from Livorno, where he was born in 1831, while he was still a young man, following in the steps of his father, Pandia; there he had started a banking business, first on his own, and then together with his cousin, Michael Rodocanachi (son of Emmanuel).

2 He may have been a pupil of some *patron* of the École des Beaux Arts, an institution which was then enjoying a moment of great prestige and which, in some ways, served as a link between the French academic tradition and certain representatives of the Modern movement, which was gaining ground in Paris in those years. One hypothesis is that he was encouraged to follow this path, and to develop his vocation, by Emmanuel Rodocanachi, who belonged to a collateral branch of the family who had settled early in Paris, where Emmanuel was born in 1859. This brilliant individual had devoted himself to historical studies, without, however, neglecting the financial business managed by his family, and he had made such a name for himself that he became a full member of the Académie Française. At this particular time, Emmanuel (who was older than Paul by ten years) was writing a study of the architecture of the Campidoglio, which was published shortly afterwards by Hachette, and he was preparing to embark on a full study of the urban transformation of Rome during the pontificates of Julius II and Leo X. Cf. E. Rodocanachi, *Le Capitole romain antique et moderne: la citadelle, les temples, le Palais sénatorial, etc.*, Hachette, Paris, 1904, and *Le trasformazioni di Roma ai tempi di Giulio II e di Leone X*, s.l., no date (but 1911). E. Rodocanachi would complete this cycle of research by publishing *Les monuments antiques de Rome encore existants, etc.*, Hachette, Paris, 1920.

3 Deed dated September 11, 1903. *Conservation des hypothèques de Fontainebleau. Sixième bureau des Hypothèques de la Seine*, vol. 65, no. 6, recorded September 29, 1903.

4 The professional architect was Émile Dameron, "architecte vérificateur, expert près les Tribunaux de Corbeil." For the building permit, see Mairie de Neuilly-sur-Seine, Service Urbanisme, dossier "Hôtel Arturo Lopez."

5 It is different, to a certain extent, from what can be seen today, also because the original entrance was through the east façade, which was topped by a tympanum crowned with a deer, overlooking a *cour d'honneur* (formal courtyard) which no longer exists. For a more detailed description of the 1903 project, see the drawings that were presented to the city council to request a building permit, or read the description made by the notary when the building was sold on November 5, 1928. *"Un hôtel particulier et ses dépendances sis à Neuilly-sur-Seine (Seine) à l'angle de la rue du Centre et de la rue de Longchamp avec pan coupé de huit mètres à l'intersection de ces deux rues, d'une contenance d'environ 5034 m2 complètement entourés de murs et grilles, avec deux grilles d'entrée sur la rue du Centre, l'une portant le n° 12, l'autre le n° 14 et une porte cochère sur la rue Longchamp sous le n° 68.*

Cette propriété comprend un bâtiment principal formant l'hôtel élevé sur partie de caves, d'un rez-de-chaussée, d'un premier étage, d'un deuxième étage sur lambris avec partie en terrasse.

Un bâtiment d'écurie comprenant huit boxes et trois chambres au premier étage. Un petit bâtiment d'un rez-de-chaussée renfermant un chenil agencé, une cuisine d'écurie et une chambre.

Un bâtiment comprenant au rez-de-chaussée une sellerie de travail, une sellerie de boxe et au premier étage grenier à fourrage.

Un bâtiment formant l'angle des rues de Longchamp et du Centre, élevé en partie sur caves d'un rez-de-chaussée avec salon, loge, salle à manger, cuisine et chambre et d'un premier étage avec deux chambres, salles de bains et water-closets. Jardin planté et dessiné dans le reste de la propriété.

Le bâtiment d'hôtel comprend: au rez-de-chaussée, cuisine, office, salle à manger des domestiques, chambre de domestiques, boudoir, deux chambres à coucher et deux cabinets de toilette, deux water-closets, au premier étage, salon, salle à manger, fumoir, trois chambres à coucher et trois cabinets de toilette, salle de bains et deux water-closets, au deuxième étage, six chambres à coucher, salle de bains et water-closet.

Le tout tenant à la rue de Longchamp par une façade de 89,98 m.

À la rue du Centre par une façade de 55,92 m.

Et d'autre part: D'un côté par une ligne parallèle au boulevard de la Seine à Madame Prat ou ses représentants sur une longueur de 300,82 m. Et d'autre côté à divers sur une longueur de 43 m." Details taken from *Documentation S.C.P. Escargueilet Bouvat-Martin, November 5, 1928.*

6 Claud writes that Bertie attended the lectures given by Henri-Louis Bergson at the Sorbonne. But the French philosopher was never appointed to the Sorbonne, although he had submitted an application first in 1894 and again in 1898. H-L. Bergson did lecture, for a five-year period, at the École Normale Supérieure, where he held the position of Maître de Conférence in 1898, but Bertie could not have heard his lectures then because he would have been too young. It seems more likely that it was Paul Rodocanachi who attended the lectures and then passed on the key information to his pupil. In this case, Bertie might well have heard Bergson lecture at the Collège de France, where he held the Chair in Modern Philosophy.

Bergson's message would certainly have attracted a restless young man like Bertie, who was driven to explore topics relating to the exercise of individual freedom, the relations between the soul and the body, the meaning of life, and, by necessity therefore, also the role of the sciences. The fact that some of Bergson's most convinced supporters regarded the philosopher as an irrationalist (in the same way as all his opponents did), or an intuitionist, or even an enemy of scientific knowledge, is sufficient to explain how Bertie could, by following Bergson, have developed the conviction that intellectual categories were useless, or worse misleading, in the search for the meaning of life. However, it was from *Matter and Memory* (Bergson's best known work at the time) that Bertie may have acquired his awareness of the pragmatic nature of intellectual consciousness, which governed many of his actions.

7 On the strength of this talent, Roger Quilter had immediately become famous in London when Denham Price had sung a song at the Crystal Palace in 1901, which Quilter had composed almost on a whim, *Song of the Sea*. The success of a new song cycle (which he had the foresight to dedicate to one of the greatest tenors of the time, Gervase Elwes) confirmed his standing as one of the most widely recognized composers among the many who crowded the English theaters during this period.

8 Marcel Proust, *In Search of Lost Time. Vol 4: Sodom and Gomorrah*, translated by Scott Moncrieff, Terence Kilmartin, D.J. Enright, Random House, 2010, p. 165: "To be sure, this is not always the case, and when, with the prodigious flowering of the Russian Ballet, revealing one after another Bakst, Nijinsky, Benois and the genius of Stravinsky, Princess Yourbeletieff, the youthful sponsor of all these new great men, appeared wearing on her head an immense, quivering aigrette that was new to the women of Paris and that they all sought to copy, it was widely supposed that this marvellous creature had been imported in their copious luggage, and as their most priceless treasure, by the Russian dancers"; see also Marcel Proust, *A la recherche du temps perdu, IX, Sodome et Gomorrhe*, (Première Partie), Nfr, Gallimard, Paris, 1921–1924, p. 184.

9 This event was *The Masque of War and Peace*, written by L.N. Parker, with music by Hamish MacCunn, which had been organized in support of charity by the wife of Arthur Paget. The performance consisted of two parts: the first included eleven *tableaux vivants*, each of which represented *A Dream of Fair Women*. The costume that Catherine wore was designed to evoke *The Five Senses*, after Titian. Two fine photographs of the Baroness survive, taken in the photographic studio of Lafayette Ltd, 179 New Bond Street, London.

10 An interesting description of the constant stream of visitors is given by one of Catherine's neighbors, who later became a successful writer: cf. Enid Bagnold's *Autobiography*, Heinemann, London, 1969, in particular pp. 102–113.

11 The d'Erlangers promptly produced an interesting commission for this young Hungarian artist, whom they had met in Paris in 1899: the portrait of Comtesse Jean de Castellane. For her part, while urging the management of Thomas Agnew & Sons to exhibit a portrait of the Grand Duke von Saxe-Weimar in its gallery, Catherine tried to organize a personal exhibition of László's work in Paris. Then she persuaded him to come to London. Here, in 1900, László drew his first portrait of her, in red chalk, to exalt the surprising color of her hair, which surrounded the perfect features of her face like a flaming red cloud. Before long, László had become Sargent's successor. He was the only artist by whom royalty and aristocrats, both in Britain and abroad, wished to be portrayed, in the hope that his art would help their image to survive.

12 Paul Morand, *Tender Shoots,* translated by Euan Cameron, Pushkin Press, 2011, p. 33.

13 Ibid., p. 42.

14 Ibid., p. 44.

15 There is an unusual witness of this activity. One day, Steve Runciman, who had decided to visit Catherine on the advice of friends, found her busy painting another leading female society figure, whom Elisabeth hated (also because Marcel Proust had made—one too many, in her opinion—appreciative remarks about her literary works). Princess Marthe Bibesco was, in the eyes of the "red duchess," too beautiful, too sophisticated, too closely linked to sovereigns and crowns: in short, too conventional. However, rather than the identity of her sitter, what is enlightening about this description of Catherine's behavior is that she used her bathroom as a painting studio. The only document to record Catherine's artistic activities is an exhibition leaflet dating from 1931 for an event held at Claridge Gallery, London, in aid of St John's Hospital. Of the thirty-eight portraits on show, six were of members of the d'Erlanger family. Among the others were portraits of Osbert Sitwell, Serge Lifar, Monsieur Leger, Paul Morand, and Cecil Beaton—all individuals whom we will meet again later in this story.

16 The portrait of Yvonne Landsberg, which Matisse made in 1914, was sold the following year at the exhibition of his work held by the Montross Gallery. It was purchased by Louise and Walter Arensberg, who later donated it to the Philadelphia Museum of Art in 1950. Cf. Anne d'Harnoncourt, A.E. Gallatin and the Arensbergs: "Pioneer Collectors of Twentieth-Century Art," *Apollo,* July 1974, pp. 52–53. Of the numerous preparatory sketches, the one owned by Bertie would be sold by the latter to the Museum of Modern Art in New York. Another was brought to my attention by Bruce Chatwin who sent me a reproduction in a letter dated October 4, 1979; he wrote that, "I have never seen another copy other than the one Bertie gave me." (On the back of the drawing, which he gave to Yvonne, Matisse had written "hommages respectueux" [best regards].) Other preparatory sketches are preserved at MoMA and at the Philadelphia Museum of Art.

17 We know—once again from Claud's account—that at some point in his life (and I suppose this was it) Bertie met his father again. The latter, having seen that Europe's political equilibrium was being jeopardized, decided to return to Brazil. In doing so, he was also counting on being able to remedy a personal financial setback in which he "had played his hand a little too carelessly on the London Stock Exchange." Claud continued, writing in Italian, "Bertie found himself employed in his father's office at Rio de Janeiro: it was a life devoid of any attraction [for him].... Therefore, after a period of work, which deprived him of all the pleasures that he come to appreciate, Bertie—who had by then saved up some money—secretly found a berth, as a simple sailor, on a ship leaving for Europe."

18 This description is taken from Lydia Sokolova's own account, *Dancing for Diaghilev,* edited by Richard Buckle, John Murray, London, 1960; also published in *Omaggio ai disegnatori di Diaghilev 1909– 1929,* Catalogue of the Exhibition for Venice realized by the Theatre Museum of London, edited by Richard Buckle, Palazzo Grassi, Venice, 1975, p. IX.

19 This was Villa Foscarini, in Stra.

20 The large poplar is the same tree that Pietro Fragiacomo had drawn a decade earlier, in 1914, beside the Palladian building, in that large painting titled *I Superstiti* (Galleria nazionale d'arte moderna, Collezioni del XIX secolo, General Catalogue inv. no. 3407). The term *palazzo* was commonly used in the seventeenth and eighteenth centuries to refer to Palladio's construction.

21 G.M. Cantacuzino, *Palladio,* Cartea Românească, Bucharest, 1928, pp. 60–61 (English translation of this passage by Lucinda Byatt). For an even earlier description of this building, and of its condition, see also Robert Henard, *Sous le cielvénitien,* Lucien Laveur Éditeur, Paris, 1911, p. 261 ff.

22 At this time, this took the form of a twin-span revolving bridge, which had been designed in 1865 by the engineer Bragato. For an image, see the study by Michele Questioni published in 2000 in *Galileo,* the magazine of the Ordine degli Ingegneri di Padova.

23 The Palladian *fabbrica* had been requisitioned by the Italian Navy in the autumn of 1917, after the disastrous retreat from Caporetto, and turned into the headquarters of the *Arditi,* the Italian army's special assault corps, which had set up camp a little further south of La Malcontenta (this was also the site of major infrastructure constructions to provide the necessary munitions for the Italian fleet engaged in the Adriatic).

24 Jean-Louis of Faucigny-Lucinge, *Un gentilhomme cosmopolite. Mémoires*, Perrin, Paris, 1990, p. 152.

25 The water was drawn from an artesian well located to the north of the *barchessa*, on its eastern side. It was then pumped using an autoclave up to the top floor of the villa, where it was stored in a zinc-plated tank.

26 In the visitors' book, Annina Morosini wrote: "malcontento è coluiche non ha visto Malcontenta!!" ("Unhappy is he who has not seen La Malcontenta!!").

27 Letter from Serge Diaghilev to Boris Kochno, August 7, 1926: Boris Kochno, *Diaghilev and the Ballets Russes*, translated by Adrienne Foulke, Harper & Row, New York, 1970, p. 222. Cf. *Omaggio ai disegnatori di Diaghilev*, op. cit., p. XI.

28 Cf. Andrea Palladio, *I Quattro Libri dell'architettura*, De Franceschi, Venice, 1570, L. II, cap. XIV, p. 50.

29 See Cesco Chinello, "Piero Foscari," *Dizionario Biografico degli Italiani*, Istituto della Enciclopedia Italiana, Treccani, Rome, 1997, vol. 49.

30 Cf. Francesco Foscari, *Dispacci da Roma, 1748–1750*, edited by Fausto Sartori, La Malcontenta, Venice, 2002; and Francesco Foscari, *Dispacci da Costantinopoli*, 1757–1762, edited by Filippo Maria Paladini, La Malcontenta, Venice, 2007.

31 Cf. Ferigo Foscari, *Dispacci da Pietroburgo, 1783–1790*, edited by Gianni Penzo Doria, introduction by Giorgetta Bonfiglio Dosio, La Malcontenta, Venice, 1993; and Ferigo Foscari, *Dispacci da Costantinopoli, 1792–1796*, edited by Franca Cosmai and Stefano Sorteni, introduction by Paolo Preto, 2 vols, La Malcontenta, Venice, 1996.

32 Lady Alexandra Colebrook also owned a residence in Venice: to be precise, in Calle del Dose, not far from San Maurizio.

33 The other members were: Lady Abdy, Baroness de Meyer, Mrs Bernstein, Countess Zoppola, Marquess of Portago, Monsieur de Beistegui, Mr Branca, and Count Celani.

34 The group was made up of Mr Mowinckle, Mr Colefax, Lady Davis, Mr Lindsay, and Misses Mary and Agnes Clarke.

35 This is evident from the fact that, in response to Catherine's request for gifts for the lottery she was organising, they only offered an old goblet and a lady's umbrella (although Bertie hastened to point out that it was made by the famous manufacturers, Briggs of London, so as not to debase the value of his gift).

36 The *stanza grande* that opened onto the terrace to the east of the building was divided by half-height partitions to create cubicles. These were used to accommodate the servants, as can be seen in the survey published in E. Forssman, *Visible Harmony, Palladio's Villa Foscari at Malcontenta*, The Swedish Museum of Architecture, Stockholm, 1973, p. 74.

37 According to one of Claud's stories, Bertie allowed himself to be photographed, but then demanded that Cecil Beaton give him the negative. Only by reading Beverley Nichol's description of the tattoos on Bertie's chest and back is it clear that such photos could clearly not be circulated: "Bertie's body was covered from head to foot with a pattern of tattoos of quite exceptional obscenity. I cannot recall them in detail because the only occasion when he revealed them to me, on a sultry afternoon in a bedroom of the Villa Malcontenta, a fleeting glance was more than enough. His chest portrayed a couple of negresses in a position which no ladies should assume, either on one's chest or anywhere else. The most shocking mural—if it can be so described—was printed into his back. When he turned round one saw a weird hunting scene, of excessive indecency, in which a troop of nymphs and satyrs were chasing a sort of fox, whose tail was vanishing up his behind." Cf. Beverley Nichols, *The Unforgiving Minute*, W.H. Allen, London, 1978, p. 158.

38 Translator's note: Two of the main protagonists in Torquato Tasso's *Gerusalemme liberata* (1581).

39 Paul Morand, *Venises*, Nrf, Gallimard, Paris, 1971, p. 111.

40 Ibid.

41 José Maria Sert, a renowned Catalan painter (the "Tiepolo of the Ritz") and choreographer, had become famous in Paris also for his eccentricity; for example, for the sombrero and Spanish cape which he wore, for his consumption of alcohol and morphine, and for his inexhaustible passion for women. He married Misia, as soon as the latter had divorced from Edwards in 1909. In 1925, without leaving "Princess Yourbeletieff" (to use the pseudonym given to Misia by Proust), Sert formed a union with a real princess, Roussanda Mdivani—known as Roussy—who was thirty years younger than him (and therefore thirty-three years younger than Misia). The result was an "absolutely theatrical" *ménage à trois* (as Cocteau described it). Indeed,

it inspired two plays: the first, in 1933, by Alfred Savoir (initially titled La donneuse, to celebrate Misia's extraordinary capacity for giving), and the second, in 1940, Cocteau's own Les monstres sacrés. This ménage à trois, with two women who succeeded in maintaining a tricky but lasting balance, and an exuberant man, in some ways forms a pendant for the threesome formed by Bertie, Catherine, and Paul. Cf. Arthur Gold and Robert Fitzdale, Misia. The Life of Misia Sert, Knopf, New York, 1980.
42 A legend started at the Venice Golf Club states that Giuseppe Volpi created the Degli Alberoni golf course to please Henry Ford. An overly sarcastic quip made by Winston Churchill was not very well received by the members of this golf club: he is alleged to have said that golf would be a beautiful sport, if it didn't have such stupid rules. Elsa Maxwell asserted that she was the first person to suggest building a golf course, when she outlined the proposal to the Mayor of Venice.
43 These descriptions are taken from a letter from Norah Lindsay. They draw attention to this interesting aristocratic English-woman, who is introduced by Allyson Hayward, her biographer, as: "Norah Lindsay, née Bourke, socialite ... and quick wit," cf. Allyson Hayward, Norah Lindsay. The life and art of a garden designer, Frances Lincoln, London, 2007, p. 7. It is also worth noting, in the context of these notes, that Norah Lindsay was related to Diana Cooper (to whom she was aunt, having married the brother of Violet Lindsay), as well as the fact of her early meeting with Catherine (they met at the Royal Dance held in honor of the Prince of Wales in 1921), her esteem for Bertie Landsberg and, later, her frequent visits to La Malcontenta as a paying guest.
44 In these circumstances, the fact that Hélène Soutzo introduced herself as Madame Verdurin was seen as a genuine act of devotion to Proust. Shortly afterwards, Princess Soutzo married Paul Morand, who appeared at that ball dressed as a dazed Baron de Charlus.
45 Cf. "L'hôtel de M. Paul Rodocanachi à Saint-James," Art et industrie, August 1926, pp. 19–21.
It is interesting to include a passage from the text published above, in which Paul Rodocanachi is described "à la fois l'architecte et décorateur" (both architect and decorator) of his own house.
"Beaucoup d'éléments anciens (parquets, boiseries, cheminées) ont été employés

dans cette construction, mais alors que tant d'autres n'ont souvent réussi qu'à réaliser un mauvais pastiche, M. Rodocanachi a su donner à cette demeure, par un juste sens des proportions et des valeurs, le caractère des beaux hôtels du XVIIIe siècle, et pour ainsi dire, à en créer toute l'atmosphère. Quelle sobre élégance dans cet escalier de pierre aux murs veinés de noir; une lanterne monumentale en fait tout le décor, et par une porte donnant sur un balcon, on aperçoit en perspective le salon et la salle à manger. Voici la galerie de musique, dont les pilastres aux peintures polychromes encadrent de hautes glaces; au fond, un piano en forme de clavecin sur lequel repose une impassible divinité. La même harmonie de proportion se retrouve dans ce salon aux boiseries d'un gris bleuté, où les fenêtres sont à peine voilées par un décor de soie transparente, et dans cette salle à manger peinte en tons marbrés avec une fantaisie et une variété délicieuse. Au rez-de-chaussée, une suite de pièces intimes forment les "petits appartements"; comment ne pas être séduit par cette bibliothèque en boiseries Louis XVI, avec des panneaux délicatement sculptés qui s'enlèvent en blanc sur un fond gris; des stores à l'italienne, en soie bleue, descendent des fenêtres, et des rideaux semblables glissent sur les rayons de la bibliothèque où miroitent des reliures précieuses.
La salle de bains est une des curiosités de l'hôtel: la baignoire en cuivre, d'époque Louis XIV, avec des robinets de bronze ciselé, est placée dans une alcôve de glaces où se reflètent les arbres du jardin. Sur le carrelage, d'un rouge vif, quelques meubles du XVIIIe siècle achèvent de donner tout son caractère à cette pièce d'un archaïsme charmant."
46 This undertaking, which was estimated to be worth 40,000 francs, is mentioned in the deed of sale, which was stipulated on November 5, 1928. Cf. Documentation S.C.P. Escargueil et Bouvat-Martin, 5 novembre 1928.
47 This contract was drawn up before the notaries Meaux and Poisson.
The purchase price of the property was 2,750,000 francs.
48 Arturo-José's collection of jewels and gold would be sold in Monaco at an auction by Sotheby's in 1992. The quality was such that many of the items were bought by the Musée du Louvre. In 1968, at the time of the sale of the house in Rue du Centre,

the French state acquired the entire furnishings of the main salon (plus a few other
armchairs) for the Chateau de Versailles.
49 Cecil Beaton, *The Glass of Fashion*,
Cassell, London, 1954, pp. 277–8.
50 Luigi Conton was a pioneer in the
research and study of Venetian ceramics
of the fifteenth and sixteenth centuries.
Cf. Luigi Conton, *Le antiche ceramiche
veneziane scoperte nella Laguna*, Fantoni,
Venece, 1940.
51 Claud added a few other details to
describe this curious solution. The low
platform on which the mysterious armchair
was placed, covering the commode, was
meant to evoke a much larger platform,
complete with wheels and draped in
a sumptuous carpet, which was used by
Princess Galitzin after her legs had been
paralysed by illness. By pushing and pulling
the platform, the princess's servants could
move it around her vast palace in St Petersburg, while she remained seated on top.
52 Marco Boschini, *La carta del Navegar
pitoresco, Edizione critica con la "Breve
Istruzione" premessa alle "RiccheMinere"
della pittura veneziana (Venezia 1660)*,
edited by Anna Pallucchini, Istituto per
la collaborazione culturale, Venice–Rome,
1966, p. 393.
53 Bernard Berenson, *Sunset and Twilight
from the Diaries of 1947–1958 (1951–
in his 87th year)*, Harcourt, Brace & World,
New York, 1963.
54 Marco Boschini, *op. cit.*, p. 393.
55 It is tempting to think that it was in front
of these giant figures that Bertie expounded
to Beverley Nichols—who had already
caught sight of the obscene images
tattooed on his body—his theories on art or,
rather, the right way to understand a work
of art: "Most historians of art begin with the
œuvre and then, if they are interested
enough, go on to discuss the sexual implications. El Greco is the most obvious example
of this. A great deal of nonsense has been
written about El Greco's sexual inclinations,
which should be obvious to any intelligent
child. I reverse this procedure. I begin with
the sex and work backwards so that when
I examine the end product I have a clear
conception of what the artist was trying to
say and why he said it in that particular manner." Cf. Beverley Nichols, *The Unforgiving
Minute*, op. cit., p. 157.
56 Bertie Landsberg, "An historic Italian
villa. Malcontenta – I. II. Venice",
Country Life, October 16 and 23, 1937,
pp. 396–401 and pp. 420–425.

57 Cf. Micaela dal Corso, "Le giornate
di Gian Battista Zelotti. Procedimenti
esecutivi della decorazione ad affresco di
una fabbrica palladiana," *Arte Documento.
Rivista e Collezione di Storia e tutela dei
Beni Culturali*, no. 27, Marcianum Press,
Venice, 2011, pp. 88–91.
58 Osbert Sitwell, *Winters of Content
and Other Discussions on Mediterranean
Art and Travel*, Duckworth & Co., London,
1932, pp. 60–87.
59 M.J.E. Felix de Rochegude, *Guide
pratique à travers le vieux Paris*, (Hachette
1897), Librairie Ancienne E. Champion,
Paris, 1923.
60 Cf. Bruce Chatwin, "Lament for
Afghanistan," in *What am I doing here?*
Cape, London, 1989, p. 286.
61 Robert Byron, *The Road to Oxiana*,
Oxford University Press, 1982 (first
published 1937), p. 19. It is worth noting that
this visit by Robert Byron and Serge Lifar
to La Malcontenta is not recorded in
Bertie's visitors' book. This confirms that
the "book" only gives a partial view of what
happened at the *palazzo*.
62 Ibid., p. 20. The villa was only connected
to the electricity mains in 1950.
63 For a more detailed picture of this
fascinating woman, see Philip Ziegler, *Diana
Cooper. The biography of Lady Diana
Cooper*, Hamish Hamilton, 1981, and also
the biography written by her son, John Julius
Norwich (ed.), *The Duff Cooper Diaries,
1915–1951*, Weidenfield and Nicolson,
1966. Lady Diana's name is included here
to recall the fact that she was related
to Norah Lindsay, who was a regular visitor
to the Palladian *palazzo* at Malcontenta.
64 Robert Byron, *op. cit.*, pp. 20–21.
65 The episode was recalled by John
McEwen, in a short tribute written to
Millington-Drake. From here, it is cited by
Nicholas Shakespeare, *Bruce Chatwin*,
Harvill, London, 1999, p. 110.
66 Beverley Nichols, *Down the Garden
Path*, Jonathan Cape, London, 1932, p. 11.
67 Known as Viscount Eric Duncannon,
he was the 10th Count of Bessborough,
Frederick Edward de Neuflize Ponsonby.
68 These quotations are taken from a letter
from Norah Lindsay to her sisters, which
was kindly drawn to my attention by Allyson
Hayward. It is from this correspondence
that we learn that Norah Lindsay first met
Catherine d'Erlanger in 1921 at a lunch with
Winston Churchill. See Allyson Hayward,
Norah Lindsay, op. cit., p. 75.

69 Victor Hugo, *Les Orientales*, Charpentier, Paris, 1841, Preface, p. 6.
70 Cf. Antonio Foscari, "Le Corbusier a Venezia nel luglio del 1934. Un Entretien, Giuseppe Volpi e altriincontri," *Ateneo Veneto. Rivista di Scienze, Lettere ed Arti. Atti e memorie dell'Ateneo Veneto*, CXCIV, 3rd series 6/II (2007), Venice, 2008, pp. 217–242; and Antonio Foscari, "À Venise en 1934", in *L'Italie de Le Corbusier*, XVe Rencontre de La Fondation Le Corbusier, Editions de La Villette, Paris, 2010, pp. 200–209.
71 Ibid.
72 Caio de Mello Franco (1896–1955), graduated in law (1918) and entered the diplomatic service; he served in Rome, as part of the mission to the Holy See, in Paris, in The Hague and in London. As Minister Plenipotentiary he represented Brazil in Ecuador (1941), Canada (1942), and Egypt (1945). He was appointed ambassador to India (1949), Peru (1952) and Paris (1953), where he died. His volumes of poetry include: *Urna* (1917), *Vida que Passa* (1924), *Cheiro de Terra* (1949), and prose works are: *O Inconfidente Clàudio Manuel da Costa* (1931), *O Parnaso Obsequioso e as Cartas Chilenas* (1931), and *Via Latina* (1933).
73 "The film taken at La Malcontenta very successful," letter from Caio de Mello Franco to Le Corbusier, August 17, 1934 (FLC U3-17-6).
74 Letter from Le Corbusier to Catherine d'Erlanger, September 12, 1934 (FLC U3-17-13).
75 Presentation given by Le Corbusier at the conference *L'art et la Réalité*, in *Entretiens. L'art et la Réalité. L'art et l'État*, Institut International de Coopération Intellectuelle, Dépôt pour la France Librairie Stock, Paris, 1934, p. 76.
76 "As soon as I returned, I went to see the shipper who showed me the bill of shipping in his records for 'Précisions,' Special Issue on Contemporary Architecture, two drawings Rio de Janeiro, dated 20 August," letter from Le Corbusier to Caio de Mello Franco, September 13, 1934.
77 The day after visiting La Malcontenta, Le Corbusier returned to Paris but, excited by all that he had seen, he promised to come back to Venice, as we learn from a letter written to him by the Greek Consul General in Venice, Typaldo Forestis, who, from 1925 onwards, was a frequent visitor to the banks of the Brenta. In order to convince Le Corbusier to undertake the journey as soon as possible, the diplomat wrote that: "Venice will be beautiful from Wednesday onwards, once the motorboats have been silenced on the lagoon, when the snobs have left, when we will be able to enjoy the wonderful sunsets of autumn." The letter then concludes: "I hope to see you soon," adding, "but with a delicious plate of spaghetti at our table." This last remark may allude to the disappointment often felt by anyone sitting down to dine with Bertie at La Malcontenta. Letter from Typaldo Forestis to Le Corbusier, September 16, 1934.
78 It was a house of great dignity, although not exactly beautiful. Having been refurbished rather pompously after the War, it is now a small hotel, which is said to be pleasant.
79 Letter from Le Corbusier to Rex Martienssen, July 27, 1939 (FLC E2-14-596).
80 Letter from Le Corbusier to A. Everett Austin, October 1, 1936 (FLC R3-04-337).
81 Ibid.
82 Bertie Landsberg was so convinced that these frescos should be attributed to Battista Franco, on account of both for their design and their execution, and he was so gifted in the art of persuasion, that for years many scholars never questioned his theory. To some extent Wittkower shared Bertie Landsberg's passion for this iconographical cycle; on August 20, 1935, he sent a series of reproductions of engravings by Battista Franco, which he had found in the British Museum, together with a list of the *Gigantomachie* conserved in the Print Room in Berlin. (It is worth noting that, with the exception of this correspondence, there is no other evidence of Wittkower'svisit to La Malcontenta. Like Robert Byron, Wittkower did not sign the visitors' book).
83 Letter from Rudolf Wittkower to Bertie Landsberg dated August 20, 1935.
84 Rudolf Wittkower, *Architectural Principles in the Age of Humanism*, Alec Tiranti Ltd., London, 1949; see, in particular, the third section: "Principles of Palladian architecture" (ed. Laterza 1964, pp. 63–146). It is interesting to note that in his book, Rudolf Wittkower illustrates the *fabbrica* built by Palladio on the banks of the Brenta with a photo dating from 1926–27, probably provided by Bertie Landsberg.
85 This visit, which lasted a few days, is reported in De Lászłó's diary. He was dyslexic, but records the following notes: "3 Sept – Tuesday went into Venise [sic] from Malcontenta – by train & Boat – it took

40 m. beautiful[l]y sousing [sic, i.e. "sooth-ing"] is the sea—& the charm of Venise—from the distance—when only the outlines are visible—no—letter of Putti's as he promised—stayed here—lived a leasures [sic] day—to Tea—Catarina d'Erlanger [sic, i.e. "Catherine d'Erlanger"] came—sur-rounded—with all her young friends—amongst them was—young Cunnard [sic, i.e. "Cunard"?] banal—The clever ordinary looking Herald [sic, i.e. "Harold" Nicolson] —Baba—the dicipated [sic, i.e. "dissi-pated"]—vulgar looking daughter of Catarina d'E. married princess Lucinge—her two little girl[s]—The daughter—of Toscanini—very attracktive [sic]—& a few more—modern—youngsters—but all interesting" (p. 103); "He accompanied us to Venise—Their [sic] was alas—Catharina—who's [sic] lover L. is—gave flowers to Lucy—!—& a kiss—!! & while we were in Malcontenta—for which she was responsi-ble!—she did not invited [sic] us—once to her strange Venetian House—for a meal—Hers—& L.'[s] view on life—is upside down!" (p. 108).

86 *Frivolitas divina* was the motto that Paul used for an *ex-libris* that Bertie was supposed to insert in the hundreds of books he had read. In order to give a playful twist to such a carefully chosen expression, Paul had designed the ex-libris with a coat of arms embellished with a mischievous figure surmounted by a cockerel (the same one which—perhaps as a reference to the chickens raised by Catherine—appeared on the letterhead paper used at La Malcon-tenta).

87 The visitors' book contains the names of some Italian scholars such as Gino Fogolari and Ferdinando Forlati, together with Bruna Forlati Tamaro, Fausto Franco, Fabio Mauroner, and Michelangelo Muraro.

88 Beverley Nichols, *The Unforgiving Minute*, op. cit., pp. 155, 156.

89 As late as June 4, 1937, the Chief Rabbi of Rome, David Prato, wrote to the Chief Rabbi of Venice, Adolfo Ottolenghi, to inform him of a meeting he had with the Foreign Minister, Galeazzo Ciano, on the previous day. "Dear Colleague, I am carrying out my duty to inform you in brief, given the approach of the Sabbath, that yesterday I had the honour of being received by His Excellency the Honourable Galeazzo Ciano for a long and pleasant talk. The declarations and assurances he gave me were sufficient to dispel any fear of a charge of heart by the government authorities in the traditionally benevolent attitude shown to Jews in Italy. As for the Zionist movement, His Excellency the Minis-ter repeatedly told me what he had declared to Dr. Goldmann.... In my opinion, it is our duty to spread calm among our communi-ties and avoid any declarations that might offend Jewish dignity and which would undoubtedly have the effect of exacerbating the situation. Even the fact of doubting our loyalty is so offensive that it would perhaps be better not to react. For us, it is sufficient that the highest authorities have made declarations concerning us, remaining within the constitutional framework of the Law on the Communities and also respect-ing our Torah. " Dr Nathan Goldmann, who is mentioned in this note, was Presi-dent of the International Jewish Community. See Renata Segre (ed.), *Gliebrei a Venezia 1938-1945. Una Comunità tra persecuzione e rinascita, Comunità Ebraica di Venezia*, doc. 4, Il Cardo, Venice, 1995.

90 See note 40.

91 The right way of bringing a building back to life, Bertie used to say, needed plenty of love, endless time, and very little money.

92 "It is interesting – Bertie would say to his friend Beverley Nichols – that such a man could produce a work of such spiritual ecstasy. Why? Because he had an insatia-ble passion for elderly gondoliers. Very elderly gondoliers." Cf. Beverley Nichols, *The Unforgiving Minute*, op. cit., p. 157.

93 In addition to Lady Diana Cooper, the other committee members were Madame de Grippenberg, Lady Ribblesdale, Lady Mendl, Lady Hamilton, Lady Davies, Norah Lindsay, Kenneth Clark, Sir Hugh Walpole, Captain Osbert Sitwell, J. Johnstone, and Rex Whistler.

94 Anna Toniolo, *Temporale a Malcontenta, sulle orme di Veronese*, in "Il Gazzettino," June 23, 1939, p. 3.

95 Maureen Emerson, *Escape to Provence*, Chapter and Verse, Sussex, 2008, p. 64.

96 Long, low farm building, typically provid-ing stabling and used to store equipment and produce.

97 Translator's note: A popular song, with Garibaldian origins, which was rewritten in the early twentieth century and adopted by the Italian Communist party: "Alla ris-cossa" means "To the revolt."

Credits

245

Antonio Foscari Widmann Rezzonico

Born in Trieste in 1938, Antonio Foscari graduated in Architecture from the University IUAV of Venice.

As an architect he has overseen the restoration of various palaces in Venice, including Palazzo Grassi (with Gae Aulenti), Palazzo Bollani (for which he received a European award), and the Teatro Malibran (after receiving an award for the competition to restore La Fenice).

Besides restoration projects, Foscari built extensively thoughout Italy (among other things he built, a research center for advanced technology in Urbino, and the Leonardo Sciascia Foundation in Sicily).

Foscari has held various public offices, mainly in Venice, including a term as President of the Accademia di Belle Arti in Venice, in which he promoted the Institute's move into the Renaissance complex of the Ospedale degli Incurabili. In recognition of his contribution to cultural affairs, he was appointed Commendatore al Merito della Repubblica by the Italian President Carlo Azeglio Ciampi.

For many years he has worked in very close collaboration with a number of French cultural organizations. In this respect, among other initiatives, he founded the *Alliance Française* in Venice, which he chaired for twenty-five years. The French Republic recognized his contributions by awarding him the *Légion d'Honneur*, nominating him to the *Ordre des Arts et des Lettres*, and lastly, appointing him as a member of the Board of Directors of the Louvre.

Foscari has been lecturing at Italian and international Universities and at the CISA (Centro Internazionale di Studi Andrea Palladio). He teaches History of Architecture at IUAV (where he is also member of the Board of Directors) and at the History and Theories Masters in the University of Roma Tre, specialising in the field of Renaissance architectural history on which he has published extensively. Amongst his publications it is worth highlighting his works in collaboration with Manfredo Tafuri, and in particular the book *L'armonia e conflitti* published by Einaudi in 1983.

Most recently, he published a monograph on Palladio, entitled *Unbuilt Venice*. The book was published by Lars Müller Publishers and was launched as a conclusion to the 500th anniversary of Andrea Palladio's birth.

Antonio Foscari,
Andrea Palladio – Unbuilt Venice,
Lars Müller Publishers, 2010

Any attempt to sum up the balance of Andrea Palladio's creative achievements is invariably distorted by the fact that some of the greatest projects of his mature years were never built.

For the most part, these unfinished works were in Venice. They include the patriarchal Church of San Pietro di Castello, the reorganization of the Rialto district at the commercial and financial heart of the city, a church that would have overlooked the Grand Canal and, lastly, the monumental complex of the monastery for the Lateran Canons, the Convento della Carità.

Antonio Foscari has restored the balance by charting the course of Andrea Palladio's remarkable life and prodigious œuvre in a way that sheds new light on all his works while also recognising a number of previously unclassified drawings.

The book culminates with an attempt, unprecedented in over 400 years of Palladian studies, to reconstruct the project that Palladio, in the autumn of his life, held to be the supreme testimonial of his creativity: the rebuilding of the Doge's Palace in Venice.

Acknowledgments

This book was conceived as a tribute to Bertie Landsberg and Claud Phillimore who taught me how to love an old house while respecting its history, and to Barbara who brought this house alive for many years, keeping its doors open both to visitors and numerous friends. But I would not have been able to write the book without Giulia's wonderful encouragement and assistance or the invaluable collaboration of Carmen Donadio. It was Pierre Rosenberg who prompted me to publish this work, which was originally intended as a memoir for Ferigo and Giulia. Benedetta Craveri, Nathan Clements Gillespie, Marilyn Perry, and Francis Phillimore were very kind and patient to read the work before print in Lucinda Byatt's exemplary translation, and offered useful comments. To them, and also to Ferigo and Claudia, and to Giulia, Philip, Georgia and Teresa, I am enormously grateful. Lars Müller has given the text the impeccable typographical finish that we have grown accustomed to expect in all his publications. Moreover, it would be remiss of me not to thank the following persons for their help during my research: Bianca Arrivabene Gonzaga, Guido Beltramini, Toto Bergamo Rossi, Laura Bossi, Howard Burns, Jean Clair, Francesco Maria Colombo, Benoît d'Aboville, Micaela Dal Corso, Fernando de Mello Franco, Florence Duruy, Maureen Emerson, Allyson Hayward, Antonio Homen, Tim Hunt, Valerie Langfield, Peter Lauritzen, David Lindsay, Jean and Marie-Françoise Loiret, Marco de Lorenzi, Diamante Luling Buschetti, Mauro Magliani, Bernard Minoret, Mitchell Owens, Miranda Phillimore, Philip Rylands, Léopold Diego Sanchez, Peggy Sharpe, Lord Snowdon, Sandro Sonino, Christopher Thomas, Francesco Turio Boehm, and Jérôme Zieseniss. I also thank the archivists, librarians and other collaborators at The Andy Warhol Foundation for the Visual Arts, Archivio Fotografico dei Musei Civici Veneziani, Archivio Storico della Celestia, Beinecke Rare Book and Manuscript Library, Biennale ASAC, Cambridge University Library, Camera Press Ltd., Collection Boris Kochno at Bibliothèque Nationale de France, Cole Porter Trust, Columbia University, Condé Nast, De László Archive Trust, Fondation Giacometti, Fondation Le Corbusier, Frances Loeb Library at Harvard University, Herbert F. Johnson Museum of Art at Cornell University, Musée du Louvre, Municipality of Neuilly-sur-Seine, Nouveau Museé National de Monaco, Yale Music Library, National Portrait Gallery, Peggy Guggenheim Collection, Robert Rauschenberg Foundation, Staatliche Kunstsammlungen Dresden, Sotheby's, and Victoria & Albert Museum.

TUMULT AND ORDER
Malcontenta 1924–1939

Antonio Foscari Widmann Rezzonico

Editorial advisor: Giulia Foscari W. R.
Editorial office: Carmen Donadio
Translations from the Italian: Lucinda Byatt
Copyediting and proofreading: Sarah Quigley
Design: Integral Lars Müller / Lars Müller and Sarah Pia
Typesetting: Integral Lars Müller / Esther Butterworth
Lithography: Ast & Fischer, Wabern, Switzerland
Printing and binding: Kösel, Altusried-Krugzell, Germany
Paper: Munken Lynx 1.13, 150 g/m²

© 2012 Lars Müller Publishers and the author

Lars Müller Publishers
Zürich, Switzerland
www.lars-mueller-publishers.com

ISBN 978-3-03778-297-2

Printed in Germany